STOLEN JUSTICE

THE STRUGGLE FOR
AFRICAN AMERICAN
VOTING RIGHTS

ALSO BY
LAWRENCE GOLDSTONE

UNPUNISHED MURDER
Massacre at Colfax and
the Quest for Justice

STOLEN JUSTICE

THE STRUGGLE FOR AFRICAN AMERICAN VOTING RIGHTS

FOREWORD BY
HENRY LOUIS GATES, JR.

LAWRENCE GOLDSTONE

SCHOLASTIC
FOCUS

NEW YORK

A NOTE TO READERS:

This book includes quoted material from primary source documents, some of which contains racially offensive language. These passages are presented in their original, unedited form in order to accurately reflect history.

Library of Congress Cataloging-in-Publication Data

Names: Goldstone, Lawrence, 1947- author.
Title: Stolen justice: the struggle for African-American voting rights / Lawrence Goldstone; foreword by Henry Louis Gates, Jr.
Description: First edition. | New York : Scholastic Focus, 2020. | Includes bibliographical references and index. | Audience: Ages 12+ | Audience: Grade 9 to 12 | Summary: "Following the Civil War, the Reconstruction era raised a new question to those in power in the US: Should African Americans, so many of them former slaves, be granted the right to vote? In a bitter partisan fight over the legislature and Constitution, the answer eventually became yes, though only after two constitutional amendments, two Reconstruction Acts, two Civil Rights Acts, three Enforcement Acts, the impeachment of a president, and an army of occupation. Yet, even that was not enough to ensure that African American voices would be heard, or their lives protected. White supremacists loudly and intentionally prevented black Americans from voting -- and they were willing to kill to do so. In this vivid portrait of the systematic suppression of the African American vote, critically acclaimed author Lawrence Goldstone traces the injustices of the post-Reconstruction era through the eyes of incredible individuals, both heroic and barbaric, and examines the legal cases that made the Supreme Court a partner of white supremacists in the rise of Jim Crow. Though this is a story of America's past, Goldstone brilliantly draws direct links to today's creeping threats to suffrage in this important and, alas, timely book"-- Provided by publisher.
Identifiers: LCCN 2019027535 | ISBN 9781338323481
Subjects: LCSH: African Americans--Suffrage--History--Juvenile literature. | African Americans--Civil rights--History--Juvenile literature. | African Americans--Segregation--History--Juvenile literature. | African Americans--Violence against--History--Juvenile literature.
Classification: LCC JK1924 .G65 2020 | DDC 324.6/208996073--dc23
LC record available at https://lccn.loc.gov/2019027535

10 9 8 7 6 5 4 3 2 1   20 21 22 23 24

Printed in the U.S.A. 23
First edition, January 2020

Book design by Becky James

TO NANCY AND LEE

TABLE OF CONTENTS

FOREWORD

MARTIN LUTHER KING, JR., GAVE his first address at the Lincoln Memorial during the Prayer Pilgrimage for Freedom on May 17, 1957. In this speech, he argued that the betrayal of disenfranchised Americans offered the best argument for why the struggle for voting rights is so essential for economic and social justice. King declared, "Give us the ballot, and we will no longer have to worry the federal government about our basic rights." In the following years, the modern civil rights movement continued its struggle for voting rights. By April 1964, Malcom X angrily expressed the frustration that many felt by the lack of progress. Ominously, he warned, "It'll be the ballot or the bullet." Indeed, by 1968, both Malcolm X and King had been assassinated, but it was King's vision of justice that came to be broadly accepted. In early 1964, the overwhelming majority of states approved the Twenty-Fourth Amendment to the Constitution, which banned the poll tax, thus finally barring economic barriers to voting. Later that year, Congress enacted the Civil Rights Act of 1964 with a comprehensive Voting Rights Act to follow in 1965.

After providing a concise and beautifully written history of enfranchisement in the United States of America, *Stolen Justice: The Struggle for African American Voting Rights* details the many ways in which voting rights were systematically denied to African Americans. Beginning this history with an account of voting privileges in the early days of the republic, Lawrence Goldstone provides a lively account of the conflicts between the Founding Fathers in their fashioning of electoral processes. To be sure, voting was a state matter, resulting in a patchwork of different rules and regimes. In all cases, slaves were excluded, but in these early days, free men of color were allowed to vote in a surprising number of states, North and South. However, the rollback was swift, especially in the South, and as the Union expanded, fewer states offered voting rights to nonwhites. Eventually, even states in the North restricted voting rights to white men. As Goldstone explains, by 1860, only a handful of Northern states allowed men of color to vote. That year New Yorkers defeated an effort to remove a property qualification that applied only to black voters. As a result, only 6 percent of free blacks in the North were registered to vote in the antebellum era.

In *Stolen Justice*, Goldstone describes the forces that led to the Reconstruction Acts of 1867–1868 and the brief period in which the vote was extended to all male freedmen over twenty-one years of age. I have seldom seen such a clear and straightforward description of the passage of the Fourteenth and Fifteenth Amendments as is presented in this book. Aiding in his historical account, Goldstone has added illustrations, photographs, and a remarkably helpful glossary of terms. Of course, the majority of *Stolen Justice* is concerned with the almost immediate attacks on the rights of African Americans following the Civil War. From the violence that began with the founding of the Ku Klux Klan within a year of Lee's surrender at Appomattox to the judicial rulings that chipped away at voting rights promised in the Fifteenth Amendment, *Stolen Justice* charts the victories of the movement to codify white supremacy in the American South. In his consideration of the judicial challenges to the Fourteenth Amendment, Goldstone begins with the compelling story of the Louisiana *Slaughter-House Cases*, in which the seemingly banal problem of where New Orleans could locate butchers ended up shifting power away from federal protections and toward state rights. Other surprising cases are cited in this volume, including *Strauder v. West Virginia* (1880), in which decisions about the racial makeup of a jury began with the case of a confessed ax murderer. In every topic cited in *Stolen Justice*, the author infuses his history with vibrant personalities, fascinating details, and outrage at racial injustice.

In the very divisive political period in which we find ourselves, it is important to remember the critical importance of voting rights for all Americans. Contemporary attempts to rig voting outcomes including extreme gerrymandering of state legislative and congressional district lines, the enactment of harshly restrictive voter ID laws, draconian restraints on early voting, and the purging of voter rolls should alarm all concerned citizens. *Stolen Justice* reminds us of our ongoing responsibility to protect voting rights.

Dr. Henry Louis Gates, Jr.
Director of the Hutchins Center
for African & African American Research
Harvard University

STOLEN JUSTICE

THE STRUGGLE FOR AFRICAN AMERICAN VOTING RIGHTS

Alex Manly.

PROLOGUE

OVERTHROW

B Y AUGUST 1898, ALEX MANLY, a thin and handsome man, only thirty-two years old, had made himself into a remarkable American success story. He was a respected community leader in Wilmington, North Carolina; owned and edited the *Daily Record*, the city's most widely read newspaper; served as the deputy register of deeds; and taught Sunday school at the Chestnut Street Presbyterian Church. And, although he was the grandson of Charles Manly, a former governor of North Carolina, Manly's achievements were in no way a result of family connections.

That was because his grandmother Corinne had been one of Charles Manly's slaves.

Although he was light-skinned, with features that could easily be taken for white, Alex Manly never forgot his African American identity. In fact, the *Daily Record* was billed as "The Only Negro Daily Paper in the World." What made Manly's achievements more unusual was that, by 1898, virtually all of the gains made by African Americans in the 1870s, during Reconstruction, had been swept away by the white supremacists who had once again taken control of state governments across the South. American citizens who happened to be African American were often treated little better than when they had been slaves. Many could not work where they chose or live where they chose; they were often brutalized by whites, arrested under the flimsiest of excuses, and subjected to beatings, rape, and even murder with little or no protection from the local police or courts. In fact, it was not unusual for the local police to be among the worst offenders. And despite anything the United States Constitution may have promised, fewer and fewer African Americans in the South were still able to vote.

But Wilmington, then North Carolina's largest city, was an exception, a thriving port on the Atlantic coast that was also an outpost of racial harmony. More than eleven thousand of its twenty thousand residents were African American—former slaves or their descendants—and black men owned a variety of businesses frequented by members of both races, from jewelry stores to real estate agencies to restaurants to barber shops. Although the mayor and city council remained almost entirely white, there were black police officers and firemen.

Members of both races voted regularly and without

intimidation. African Americans voted Republican, then the party of equal rights, and exerted a good deal of influence in Wilmington. Democrats, however, the party of white supremacy, had for decades controlled the state house in Raleigh. But in 1894, North Carolina's Populist Party, a group of mostly small farmers, almost all of whom were white, had tired of the Democratic ruling elite and joined with black Republicans to force Democrats from state government.

Although almost all the whites in this coalition continued to believe in the racial inferiority of African Americans, they needed the black vote to defeat their enemies. And defeat them they did. In the November 1894 elections, Fusionists, as they called themselves, took control of the general assembly and the state supreme court, and also won in most of the state's congressional districts. Although once again the vast majority of new officeholders were white, some black men were elected to local and state office, by then almost unheard of in the South. Once in power, Fusionists made it easier for blacks and poor whites to vote, imposed taxes to fund public education, and passed a number of economic laws that favored small farmers and businessmen over large financial interests.

Democrats were enraged at these changes, but nearly all of their anger focused on the measures that improved voting prospects for black men. (Women would not gain the vote for more than two decades.) The Fusionists were again successful in 1896, even adding the governorship to their trophy case when Daniel Russell, a Wilmington native, was elected to that office. Democrats were determined to win it back.

As the 1898 elections approached, Daniel Schenck, a leading Democrat, warned, "It will be the meanest, vilest, dirtiest campaign since 1876. The slogan of the Democratic Party from the mountains to the sea will be but one word—nigger." One of the main Democratic campaign themes was that if their party were not returned to power, there would be an epidemic of attacks by black men on white women.

To stoke those fires, a statewide Democratic newspaper, the *News & Observer*, reprinted an August 1897 speech by a Georgia suffragette—a campaigner for a woman's right to vote—named Rebecca Latimer Felton, who would later become the first woman to serve in the United States Senate. "If it requires lynching to protect woman's dearest possession from ravening, drunken human beasts," she had told an enthusiastic white audience, "then I say lynch a thousand negroes a week."

Alex Manly had generally avoided controversy, but the accusation in the *News & Observer* that black men preyed on white women was too much. Manly, whose very existence was due to a white man preying on a black woman, responded with an editorial in which he charged white lynch mobs with murdering African American men because white women had *chosen* to become romantically involved with them. "Meetings of this kind go on for some time," he wrote, "until the woman's infatuation or the man's boldness brings attention to them and the man is lynched for rape. Every Negro lynched is called a 'big, burly, black brute,' when in fact many of those who have thus been dealt with had white men for their fathers, and were not only not 'black' and 'burly' but were sufficiently attractive for white girls of culture and refinement to fall in love with them, as is very well known to all."

It is difficult to imagine an accusation that would more enrage white supremacists.

Manly's editorial was reprinted across the South, accompanied by thinly disguised calls to do violence against him. Typical was an article in the *Jacksonville Times*. "Last week the editor of the Daily Record of Wilmington, the only negro daily printed in the state, published the following slander about the white women of the south. Strange to say the wretch has not been lynched, but poses before the people as one of the grand achievements of republican rule and a hideous example of one of the many that have come to the surface since white supremacy was relegated to the rear by selfish politicians."

The editorial and the fact that Wilmington had so many successful African Americans made the city perfect for Democrats to inflame white rage as the November election

"Pitchfork Ben" Tillman.

approached. When South Carolina senator "Pitchfork Ben" Tillman visited his neighboring state to campaign for white rule, he thundered to a cheering crowd, "Why didn't you kill that damn nigger editor who wrote that? Send him to South Carolina and let him publish any such offensive stuff, and he will be killed." (Tillman had acquired his nickname for threatening to stick a pitchfork into President Grover Cleveland, whom he called "a bag of beef.") Sprinkled through Tillman's audience were men dressed in red shirts, the first appearance of a group of white supremacist paramilitaries—civilians operating as if they were soldiers—determined to use any means necessary to take back state government.

At a rally on the night of November 7, 1898, the eve of the election, Alfred Waddell addressed a Red Shirt rally. Waddell was a former Confederate cavalry officer who had served three terms in Congress before losing his seat in 1878

Red Shirts.

to Daniel Russell, who at the time was a Republican. He told the Red Shirts, "You are Anglo-Saxons. You are armed and prepared, and you will do your duty. If you find the Negro out voting, tell him to leave the polls, and if he refuses, kill him, shoot him down in his tracks. We shall win tomorrow if we have to do it with guns."

With Red Shirts and other armed white men roaming the streets, Democrats regained all they had lost in the election four years before, winning in Wilmington by six thousand votes, where they had lost by five thousand votes only two years earlier. Fraud was everywhere. Ballot boxes were stuffed so openly with phony votes for Democrats that in some districts the number of votes for Democratic candidates exceeded the total number of registered voters. In one precinct, for example, although only 30 Democrats were registered, 456 Democratic votes were reported out. Another precinct, with only 343 registered voters, reported out 607 votes, almost all for Democrats. And where the white Democratic vote was inflated, Red Shirts made certain the Republican vote, especially among African Americans, was suppressed. One predominantly black precinct reported only 97 votes, although 337 Republicans had registered. The Red Shirts were so brazen that they met the train carrying Governor Russell, who was returning home to vote, and threatened to lynch him. Russell ran through the train and hid in a baggage car to escape.

Although Democrats had achieved almost total victory across North Carolina, triumph had only increased their thirst for revenge, especially in Wilmington, where Alex Manly's editorial and a thriving black community remained irresistible targets. In addition, since many local officials had not been up for reelection in 1898, Fusionists remained a power in city government.

On the morning of November 9, one day after the election, Waddell again called a meeting of Red Shirts. He waved in front of him a "White Declaration of Independence," which insisted that the American Constitution "did not anticipate the enfranchisement of an ignorant population of African origin." The Founding Fathers "did not contemplate for their descendants a subjection to an inferior race."

The following morning, Waddell, "his white hair flowing in the light breeze," led an armed band of more than one hundred white supremacists on a procession to Alex Manly's newspaper office. Manly was not there, so they stormed inside, poured kerosene on all the printing equipment, and set it ablaze. Soon, the wooden building was consumed in flames and totally gutted.

Alex Manly's charred printing press.

The soaring flames seemed only to make the rampaging white mob more furious at black residents of Wilmington, even those who lived peacefully and were not at all involved in politics.

And so the shooting began.

Rev. Charles S. Morris, a Wilmington pastor, gave an eyewitness account in a speech to the International Association of Colored Clergymen in Boston in January 1899.

> Nine Negroes massacred outright; a score wounded and hunted like partridges on the mountain; one man, brave enough to fight against such odds, who would be hailed as a hero anywhere else, was given the privilege of running the gauntlet up a broad street, where he sank ankle deep in the sand, while crowds of men lined the sidewalks and riddled him with a pint of bullets as he ran bleeding past their doors; another Negro shot twenty times in the back as he scrambled empty handed over a fence; thousands of women and children fleeing in terror from their humble homes in the darkness of the night, out under a gray and angry sky, from which falls a cold and bone chilling rain, out to the dark and tangled ooze of the swamp amid the crawling things of night, fearing to light a fire, startled at every footstep,

cowering, shivering, shuddering, trembling, praying in gloom and terror: half clad and bare-footed mothers, with their babies wrapped only in a shawl, whimpering with cold and hunger at their icy breasts, crouched in terror from the vengeance of those who, in the name of civilization, and with the benediction of the ministers of the Prince of Peace, inaugurated the reformation of the city of Wilmington the day after the election by driving out one set of white office holders and filling their places with another set of white office holders—the one being Republican and the other Democrat. All this happened, not in Turkey, nor in Russia, nor in Spain, not in the gardens of Nero, nor in the dungeons of Torquemada, but within three hundred miles of the White House.

The killing did not end until the following day. Two dozen African Americans were officially reported murdered, but scores more may have been killed and their bodies dumped into the river. One local historian, Harry Hayden, an eyewitness, insisted that more than three hundred had died.

While African Americans were slaughtered or ran in terror to hide in the nearby woods, Waddell and his men invaded city hall and informed the mayor, the aldermen, and the police chief, all Fusionists, that they must either resign on

Wilmington vigilantes posing in front of the burned-out newspaper office.

the spot or be shot down. All complied, and by late afternoon, November 10, 1898, Wilmington had a new government, led by Mayor Alfred Waddell. Those local officials, both black and white, lucky enough not to be murdered were marched to the train station, some with nooses around their necks, and told they would be killed if they ever returned. None did.

Although the white press would later term the events in Wilmington a "race riot," it was in fact the only violent overthrow of a local government in United States history.

Harry Hayden, interviewed later by reporters, insisted that he and his fellows were not thugs. "The Men who took down their shotguns and cleared the Negroes out of office yesterday were . . . men of property, intelligence, culture . . . clergyman, lawyers, bankers, merchants. They are not a mob. They are revolutionists asserting a sacred privilege and a right." North Carolina authorities evidently agreed, since no one was punished for the crimes and Waddell and his fellow Democrats were allowed to remain in the jobs they had seized by force.

As to the terrified black citizens who had been forced to flee to the woods and sleep without blankets or shelter in a cold rain, only a few attempted to sneak back to town to gather some possessions before leaving Wilmington for good. In all, more than two thousand African American men, women, and children fled the city, most of whom, like Rev.

Morris, would never return. Those who remained would live in total subjugation for the rest of their lives.

The victors, proud and triumphant, posed for a group picture in front of Alex Manly's burned-out newspaper office, which was later reproduced in newspapers and magazines across America. But they had failed in one of their main objectives—to lynch Alex Manly. Years later, Manly's son Milo described how his father had escaped.

> A German grocer, who knew my father got in touch with him, and said, 'Look, you've got to get out of town . . . This gang, there's all these people out there, but they've lined it up that nobody can leave the vicinity of this area, with this cordon, unless they have a certain pass-word.' He said, 'Now, if it ever got known that I gave you the password, they'd kill me. But I know you. I trust you. I want you to get out of here.' He gave my father the password. My father come up the line. They stopped him. 'Where are you going?' He said—named a town up there. 'What are you going up there for?' 'Going to buy some horses. There's an auction up there.' Or something like that. 'Oh, all right.' He gave the password. 'Okay, but if you see that nigger Manly up there, shoot him.' And

they gave him two rifles. That's right. Off away
he went.

North Carolina authorities, appalled at the events in
Wilmington, vowed to make certain such an incident could
never take place again. The following year, the state legislature passed an amendment to the North Carolina constitution
with provisions making it almost impossible for any African
American to vote in the state.

CHAPTER 1

WHO VOTES?

I N THE SUMMER OF 1787, when the fifty-five delegates to
the Constitutional Convention in Philadelphia were
pounding out rules for a new government, one of the most
important questions was who should be allowed to vote and
for what offices. Women, slaves, and Native Americans—still
called "Indians"—were out of the question, but what should
be required in order that a man—almost always a white
man—be allowed to participate in government?

Very few of the delegates, all white men of property themselves, favored allowing those who were not property holders
to help choose the nation's leaders. James Madison, who
would later write in *The Federalist*, "The definition of the right
of suffrage is very justly regarded as a fundamental article of
republican government," had a very different view in August
1787. In a convention session, which was kept secret from the
public, he said, "Viewing the subject in its merits alone,
the freeholders [that is, landowners] of the country would
be the safest depositories of republican liberty." John Adams,

then the nation's chief diplomat in London, was not present at the convention but had previously made his views known. In a letter written only six weeks before he would sign the Declaration of Independence, Adams expressed a firm conviction that those without property should not be allowed to vote. "Such is the frailty of the human heart, that very few men who have no property have any judgment of their own," he wrote.

Alexander Hamilton was the most insistent that only men of property could be trusted to vote in the best interests of the nation. In a 1775 pamphlet, *The Farmer Refuted*, Hamilton cited the great English legal theorist William Blackstone, who insisted that those "under the immediate dominion of others"—workers—or "persons of indigent fortunes"—the poor—could not be trusted to "give his vote freely, and without influence of any kind, then, upon the true theory and genuine principles of liberty." At the convention, Hamilton, during a six-hour speech in which he proposed a system of government very much like a monarchy, added, "All communities divide themselves into the few and the many. The first are rich and well born; the other, the mass of the people. The voice of the people has been said to be the voice of God; and however generally this maxim has been quoted and believed, it is not true in fact. The people are turbulent and changing; they seldom judge or determine right. Give therefore to the first class a distinct, permanent share in the government."

The only prominent Founder who favored allowing "universal" voting rights—at least among adult white males—was Thomas Jefferson, who in 1787 was representing the United States in Paris, and so also did not attend the Constitutional Convention. Jefferson had written in a 1776 letter, "I was for extending the rights of suffrage (or in other words the rights of a citizen) to all who had a

THE
FARMER REFUTED:
OR,
A more impartial and comprehenfive
V I E W
OF THE
DISPUTE between GREAT-BRITAIN
AND THE
COLONIES,
INTENDED AS A
FURTHER VINDICATION
OF THE
CONGRESS:
IN
ANSWER TO A LETTER
FROM
A. W. FARMER,
INTITLED
A VIEW of the CONTROVERSY
BETWEEN
GREAT-BRITAIN *and her* COLONIES:
INCLUDING
A MODE of determining the prefent DISPUTES
FINALLY AND EFFECTUALLY, &c.

Titult remedia pollicentur; fed pixidet ipfe venena continent. COKE.
The Title promifes Remedies, but the Box itfelf contains Poifons.

NEW-YORK: Printed by JAMES RIVINGTON. 1775.

Hamilton's 1775 pamphlet where he first proposed a property requirement for voting.

permanent intention of living in the country. Take what circumstances you please as evidence for this, either the having resided a certain time, or having a family, or having property, any or all of them." In a 1789 letter, he added, "Whenever the people are well-informed, they can be trusted with their own government; whenever things get so far wrong as to attract their notice, they may be relied on to set them to rights."

In the end, the convention delegates chose to avoid the issue entirely. For the House of Representatives, Article I, Section 2 simply reads that it "shall be composed of Members

chosen every second Year by the People of the several States,"
without specifying *which* people, except that qualifications
would be the same as those for "the most numerous Branch"
of a state's legislature. Senators were to be chosen entirely by
state legislatures—which was changed to popular vote in 1913
by the Seventeenth Amendment—and the president would
be chosen by "electors," equal to a state's total number of
congressmen, chosen once again according to rules adopted
by individual state governments.

Although most Americans had been left out of the voting

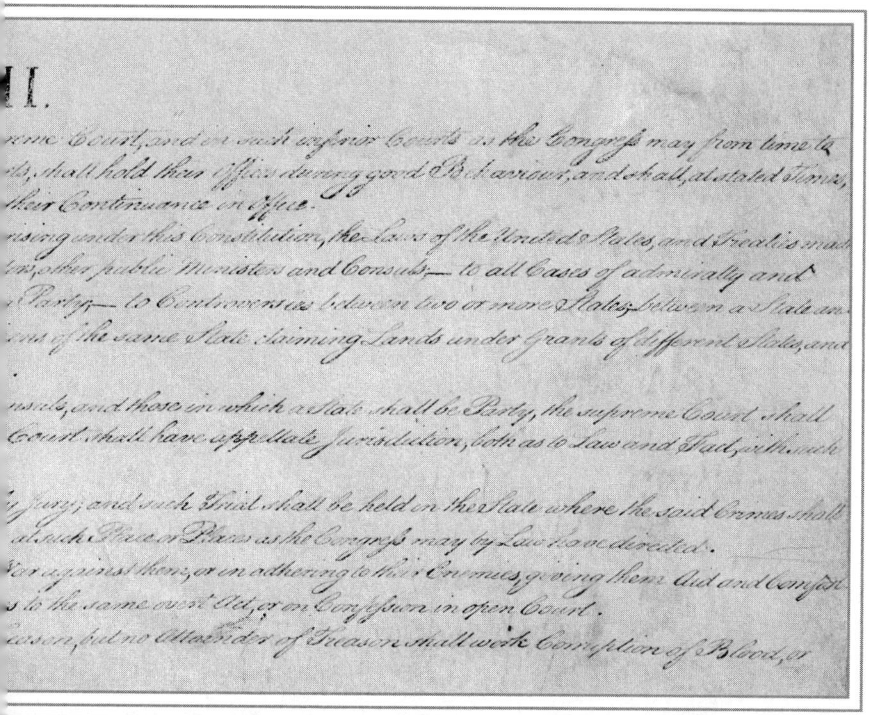

Article III contains only two brief sections.

process entirely, this was not a feature that Federalists—those who favored enacting the new Constitution—wanted to publicize during the period when the document needed to be ratified—approved—by nine of the existing thirteen states. In the *Federalist* paper number 52, for example, James Madison, after calling the right to vote "fundamental," wrote, "It was incumbent on the convention, therefore, to define and establish this right in the Constitution. To have left it open for the occasional regulation of the Congress would have been improper for the reason just mentioned. To have submitted it to the legislative discretion of the States, would have been improper for the same reason; and for the additional reason that it would have rendered too dependent on the State governments that branch of the federal government which ought to be dependent on the people alone."

In fact, almost none of this was true. The right to vote was left almost entirely "to the legislative discretion of the States," and they would exercise that right as they saw fit until after the Civil War, when the right to vote began to come under the authority of the Constitution with the enactment of the Fourteenth and Fifteenth Amendments. Although each of these amendments was meant to ensure that newly freed slaves—"freedmen"—could not be denied access to the ballot box because of the color of their skin, it would be the Supreme Court's job to decide just how far those guarantees stretched.

The Court's opinions would shape race relations in the United States for more than a century, and their impact continues to be felt across the nation today.

CHAPTER 2

HODGEPODGE

BECAUSE THE FOUNDERS HAD BEEN unwilling to take on the issue, voting across the thirteen states, and in all new states admitted to the Union, often varied as much as the states themselves. The only requirement common to every one of the original thirteen states was that a voter needed to be a property holder—in most cases showing he owned land, but in some only that he paid taxes. Some states excluded certain religions—Jews or Catholics—while others charged a fee to vote—a poll tax. Some states excluded immigrants, and every state denied the vote—also called the "franchise"—to slaves and Native Americans.

As a result, at the time of the first presidential election, which took place from Monday, December 15, 1788, to Saturday, January 10, 1789—Congress did not establish a national election day, "the Tuesday after the first Monday in November," until 1845—only *six* out of every *one hundred* Americans was eligible to vote.

In some cases, that six included African Americans. After

ratification of the United States Constitution, while no state allowed a slave to vote, the voting rights for free men of color who met a state's property requirement were surprisingly widespread. They could vote by law in Maryland, Massachusetts, Pennsylvania, and New Hampshire, and were not specifically restricted from voting in Connecticut, New York, New Jersey, Delaware, Rhode Island, and, surprisingly, North Carolina. The only states legally barring black men from voting were Virginia, South Carolina, and thinly populated Georgia.

Beginning in 1790, Congress began to define national citizenship, which would also impact access to the ballot box. That year, the first Naturalization Act allowed free white immigrants "of good character" to become United States citizens, provided they lived in the nation for two years and in their state of residence for one. Immigrants of color and Asians were excluded. In 1795, the residence requirement was extended to five years, and in 1798 to fourteen. In 1802, under President Thomas Jefferson, who wished to encourage small farmers to immigrate, the residence requirement was returned to the five-year standard, where it remains today.

Because each state was free to make its own rules, a number of quirks worked their way into the system. One of the oddest was in New Jersey, where the 1776 state constitution granted all "persons" who met the property requirement the

An Act

A BILL to establish an uniform Rule of Naturalization, and to enable Aliens to hold Lands under certain Restrictions.

Sect. 1st BE IT ENACTED BY THE SENATE AND HOUSE OF REPRESENTATIVES OF THE UNITED STATES OF AMERICA IN CONGRESS ASSEMBLED. That any alien, ~~other than an alien enemy,~~ being a free white person, who shall have resided within the limits and under the jurisdiction of the United States for the term of TWO YEARS, may be admitted to become a citizen thereof, on application to any common law court of record in any one of the States wherein he shall have resided for the term of ONE YEAR at least, and making proof to the satisfaction of such court, that he is a person of a good character, and taking the oath or affirmation prescribed by law to support the Constitution of the United States, which oath or affirmation such court shall administer, and the clerk of such court shall record such application and the proceedings thereon ; and thereupon such person shall be ~~considered as a~~ citizen of the United States. And the children of such person so naturalized, dwelling within the United States, being under the age of twenty-one years at the time of such naturalization, shall also be considered as citizens of the United States. And the children of citizens of the United States, that may be born beyond sea, or out of the limits of the United States, shall be considered as natural born citizens.

considered as a

PROVIDED, That the right of citizenship shall not descend to persons whose fathers have never been resident in the United States :

PROVIDED ALSO, That no person heretofore proscribed by any State shall be admitted a citizen as aforesaid, except by an Act of the Legislature of the State in which such person was proscribed.

[NEW YORK, ~~PRINTED BY~~ THOMAS GREENLEAF.]

Naturalization Act of 1790.

right to vote. As a result—to the horror of many men—widows and other women who owned property regularly cast ballots.

In the first decades of the nineteenth century, some uniformity finally began to appear in voting regulations across the nation. In 1807, for example, at the same time it granted the vote to all adult white males regardless of property holdings, New Jersey ended voting by women. Many of the newly admitted states had allowed adult men without property to vote, and by the 1820s, only three states—Rhode Island, Virginia, and North Carolina—still had landholding requirements. Each of those was repealed in the next decades. By 1856, both religious and property-holding requirements had been eliminated in every state in the Union, although six states continued to require that voters also be taxpayers.

But if voting rights were expanding for white men, they were narrowing for free men of color. In 1792, Delaware stripped the vote from free black men, and in 1799, when Kentucky joined the Union, it did as well. Tennessee broke the trend when it was granted statehood in 1796, allowing every free male twenty-one years old or more to vote, but Ohio, when it joined the Union seven years later, restricted the vote to white men.

During this period of expansion, some of the original colonies—Maryland, New Jersey, and New York—either outlawed African American voting or passed laws that achieved the same end. While newly admitted slave states Louisiana, Mississippi, Alabama, and Missouri did not even consider allowing free African Americans to vote, neither did free states Illinois, Indiana, Michigan, Iowa, and Oregon.

The trend of newly admitted states restricting the vote to white men, and states where African Americans had voted stripping away that right continued. By 1860, only Maine, Vermont, Massachusetts, New Hampshire, and Wisconsin opened the ballot to men of color.

As the war that would define whether or not, as Thomas Jefferson wrote, "all men were created equal," drew terrifyingly close, even free Americans of color had little or no say in deciding how to answer the question.

CHAPTER 3

TWO AMENDMENTS . . .

I N EARLY 1864, AS THE Civil War approached its third bloody anniversary and the eventual defeat of the Confederacy began to seem assured, the United States—and Abraham Lincoln—at last decided to deal with slavery. The Constitution had allowed it, the Supreme Court in *Dred Scott v. Sandford* had reinforced it, and Lincoln's Emancipation Proclamation of January 1863 had prolonged it by not freeing slaves in any state that had remained in the Union.

It took until January 1865, but then, over strong opposition from the Democratic Party, the House of Representatives, on its second try, passed by the required two-thirds vote a new amendment to the Constitution. This amendment, the Thirteenth, abolished, once and for all, in every corner of the nation, the practice of human slavery. (The Senate had approved the amendment in April 1864.) Although the president plays no official role in amending the Constitution, Lincoln had persuaded, flattered, and threatened reluctant congressmen to obtain the required majority. In December

1865, with the Confederacy a memory and President Lincoln dead, the amendment was ratified by the required three-quarters of the state legislatures and became law.

But the end of slavery did not mean the beginning of racial equality. The new president was Andrew Johnson of Tennessee, a fervent believer in states' rights and an equally fervent opponent of equal rights for freedmen. He had allowed state governments in the defeated Confederacy to be dominated by white supremacists, and to enact what became known as "Black Codes," a series of laws that denied black Americans the right to work where they pleased, live where they pleased, and often even the right of citizenship itself.

Congress fought back. In January 1866, a group of senators and representatives called "Radical Republicans," who had as deep a commitment to equal rights as the president had to white rule, forced passage of "A Bill to Protect All Persons in the United States in Their Civil Rights and Liberties."

Aimed squarely at the Black Codes, the bill proclaimed, "All persons born in the United States and not subject to any foreign power . . . are hereby declared to be citizens of the United States." Freedmen were also guaranteed the right to enter into contracts, so they might own homes and businesses; access to the legal system, so they could sue anyone who wronged them; the right to choose their own employment; and to "full and equal benefits of all laws and proceedings for the security of person and property." Denial of any of these rights became a federal crime, with violators tried in federal, not state, courts.

Andrew Johnson quickly vetoed the bill. But Congress, if two-thirds of both houses agree, can "override" a veto and make a bill law without the president's signature. On April 9, 1866, Congress did just that, and the United States had its first-ever law guaranteeing basic rights to African Americans.

But what Congress enacts, Congress can eliminate. To protect these freedoms, then, Republicans needed to put them in a place where Johnson and the Democrats could never get at them.

The Constitution.

John Bingham, a Republican congressman from Ohio, drafted what was to become one of the most vital and widely debated passages in the entire Constitution—Section 1 of the proposed Fourteenth Amendment. "All persons born or naturalized in the United States, and subject to the jurisdiction thereof, are citizens of the United States and of the state wherein they reside. No state shall make or enforce any law which shall abridge the privileges or immunities of citizens of the United States; nor shall any state deprive any person of life, liberty, or property, without due process of law; nor deny to any person within its jurisdiction the equal protection of the laws."

John Bingham.

Bingham's goal, he said later, was "a simple, strong, plain declaration that equal laws and equal and exact justice shall hereafter be secured within every State of the Union." In addition, with this amendment, the "privileges and immunities" of citizenship guaranteed in the Bill of Rights, which had originally applied only to federal law, would now also be binding on the states. While not addressing voting directly—the Civil Rights Act of 1866 had not either—few could doubt that the right to vote, at least for adult males, seemed surely to be a "privilege" of citizenship. Once again, anyone who attempted to deny the rights and guarantees of the amendment would be tried in federal court.

To become law, however, the Fourteenth Amendment would need to be ratified by three-quarters of the state legislatures. But three-quarters of what? How many states were in the Union? Were the states of the old Confederacy still part of the United States or not?

Everyone in the North, from President Lincoln on down, had insisted that secession was illegal. That meant the eleven Confederate states were still part of the Union, and therefore entitled to representation in Congress. That was how the country had functioned during the war. In 1862, 57 of the 241 seats in the House of Representatives had been granted to the eleven states that had seceded, but the seats had remained empty.

But the 1862 numbers had been arrived at by counting only

three-fifths of the slaves for apportionment, as specified in Article I, Section 2, of the Constitution. With slavery abolished, freedmen would be counted in full. The slave states would therefore retake their places in Congress with thirty-seven more seats in the House of Representatives, and thirty-seven more votes in the Electoral College, than they had when they started the most destructive war in American history.

The Thirteenth Amendment had been ratified based on the full complement of states, and increased representation was one of the reasons the former Confederate states had agreed to abolish slavery. They realized full well that they would have gained significant power in government as a result of *losing* the Civil War—but only if white people alone were allowed to vote.

Republicans were aware of what was afoot and tried to head off white Southerners with Section 2 of the proposed Fourteenth Amendment, which reduced the number of congressmen a state would be allowed if it denied the vote "to any of the male inhabitants of such State, being twenty-one years of age, and citizens of the United States." The greater percentage of adult males a state denied the vote, the more House seats the state would lose.

But there was no way that Southern states, with their white supremacist governments in place, would ratify such an amendment, and, except for Tennessee—to Andrew Johnson's fury—none did. That left the amendment well short of the required three-quarters. Republicans had no intention of changing the amendment, so instead they decided to change the state governments. And the only way to do that was with the votes of newly freed slaves.

But voting was the one basic right that even most Radical Republicans were not certain should be granted immediately. After all, most freedmen could not read or write, had no schooling or experience in citizenship, and had spent their lives existing in conditions that in no way resembled the society that freedom had made them a part of. Republicans worried that freedmen might be tricked into voting for candidates they did not really want—Democrats. As a result, Radical Republicans thought the right to vote should be granted only after freedmen had received enough education to cast their ballots wisely—and for Republicans.

But as Republicans digested Thirteenth Amendment arithmetic, this no longer mattered. Freedmen must be granted the right to vote as soon as possible, and they must cast their votes for the party that wished to protect them.

And so, in March 1867, Congress passed "An Act to Provide for the More Efficient Government of the Rebel States," which quickly became known as the "Reconstruction Act." The law divided the ten secessionist states that had refused to ratify the Fourteenth Amendment into five military districts, each commanded by no less than a brigadier general, and directed the district commanders to "protect all persons in their rights of person and property, to suppress insurrection, disorder, and violence, and to punish, or cause to be punished, all disturbers of the public peace and criminals." To achieve this, a commander could empower local courts or, if he chose, use military tribunals to deal with the offenders. Only death sentences were subject to review, and those by the president.

Each of the ten occupied states would then be required to "form a constitution . . . in conformity with the Constitution of the United States in all respects." State constitutions were to be drafted by "male citizens, twenty-one years old and upward, of whatever race, color, or previous condition." The resulting document would then need to be approved by Congress. When a state's constitution had been approved and a legislature formed, the state would be required to ratify the Fourteenth Amendment to retake its seats in Congress.

Andrew Johnson vetoed the bill almost the moment it arrived at his desk. (He had complained to a newspaperman that white Americans "were being trodden under foot to protect niggers.") Just as quickly, Congress overrode the veto.

But with white supremacist legislatures still in place, each of the remaining ten secessionist states refused to alter its constitution. So Republicans forced through another law, this one requiring the commanding general of each of the five military districts to register every male twenty-one or over to vote on whether or not to hold a state constitutional convention. The bill also gave instructions on how the conventions would be held, how the votes would be counted, and how the people counting the votes would be protected, all under the security of the army. Once again, Andrew Johnson vetoed the bill, and once again the Radical Congress overrode him.

And so, multitudes of black Americans gained access to the ballot box for the first time. Almost all would register as Republicans. In addition, to make certain there were no further barriers to reform, military governments took the vote away from any white man deemed a "rebel," almost all of whom were Democrats. Thousands of former Confederate soldiers or government officials, especially those who would not swear allegiance to the government in Washington, found themselves no longer able to cast ballots in national elections.

With newly anointed African American citizens registering to vote by the tens of thousands under the watchful eye of the army, the state constitutional conventions were approved, African Americans voting "aye" almost unanimously. New constitutions were then drafted and approved. The white supremacist governments were replaced by Republican-controlled state legislatures. Only then, in July 1868, was the Fourteenth Amendment ratified and the former Confederate states readmitted to the Union.

CHAPTER 4

... AND A THIRD: EQUAL
RIGHTS COMES TO THE
BALLOT BOX

THE RECONSTRUCTION ACTS transformed the Confederacy. Union Leagues (sometimes called "Loyal Leagues"), which promoted African American political activity, sprang up throughout the South. Freedmen registered to vote, asserted their civil and property rights, and attended schools. Thousands went to the polls, voting for the first time.

Newly empowered African Americans, both freedmen and freeborn, soon realized that they not only could vote for those seeking elective office, but could seek elective office themselves. Throughout the old Confederacy, more than two thousand people of color would hold office during Reconstruction. Almost two hundred of these would be on the federal level, including two senators, fourteen representatives, eleven United States deputy marshals, three treasury agents, and two ambassadors. There were also African American postmasters, census takers, Land Office agents, customs

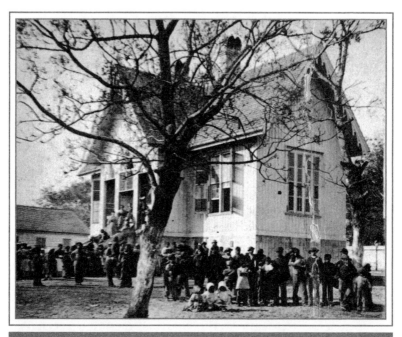
African American children stand outside their schoolhouse in South Carolina.

officials, and timber agents. On the state level, more than eight hundred served in the legislature, and three hundred were elected as delegates to constitutional conventions. There were militia officers, secretaries of state, superintendents of education, state treasurers, land commissioners, and one deputy physician in a lunatic asylum. One man, P. B. S. Pinchback, served as governor of Louisiana, if only for a few days.

The social fabric of the South also changed. Many Northerners, both black and white, traveled to the new South to participate in the great experiment of Reconstruction. Some came to make money, others because they believed deeply in equality for all people. To the white South, however, they were all "carpetbaggers," arriving only to line their pockets at the expense of a defeated nation. But white resentment aside, Reconstruction, fragile though it was, seemed just possibly on the verge of creating not only a new South, but also a new America.

But white America was growing tired of the time and money spent promoting the interests of freed slaves. In 1868, although Ulysses Grant was elected president, Democrats, promising to end or at least limit Reconstruction, made great gains, especially in the North. In fact, without the African American vote in the South, and if the former Confederates whose voting rights had been taken away had been allowed to cast ballots, Grant would likely have lost the popular vote. And all of this without three Southern states—Texas, Virginia, and Mississippi—that had not yet been readmitted to the Union. The second section of the Fourteenth Amendment, it seemed, would not be enough to maintain Republican dominance in government, especially if—or when—the army was withdrawn from the South.

Once more, the answer was in the Constitution.

With John Bingham again leading the way, Republicans

GISLATURE · 1887-1888
Griggs, W.H.Ash, B.J. Robertville

Virginia state legislators.

in Congress introduced an amendment that would prohibit denying anyone the vote on the basis of their race or "previous condition of servitude." Bingham also wanted to guarantee that freedmen would not be prevented from voting by any little tricks Southern—or even Northern—Democrats might come up with. His original proposal banned literacy tests, a poll tax, education requirements, property ownership, or birth outside the United States as reasons for denying someone the right to register to vote. But these went too far even for many Republicans, who had become uncomfortable at the prospect of their party being dominated by black skin. So Bingham settled for a stripped-down version that read simply, "The right of citizens of the United States to vote shall not be denied or abridged by the United States or by any state on account of race, color, or previous condition of servitude." In late February 1869, just one week before Democrats would increase their congressional delegations enough to block a two-thirds majority, Congress approved the amendment and sent it on to the states.

It took almost an entire year, but in early February 1870, the required twenty-eight states had ratified, and the Fifteenth Amendment became law. This included nine of the eleven Confederate states, by then with Republican legislatures. Never again, proponents proclaimed, would a person be legally denied the right to vote because of the color of his, and eventually her, skin.

But although white supremacists in the South had been denied legal means to prevent black voting—or so it seemed— they soon discovered that there were alternatives that could be every bit as effective.

Magazine cover from 1867 showing freedmen voting for the first time. Hundreds of thousands more gained the right after passage of the Fifteenth Amendment.

CHAPTER 5

POWER IN BLACK AND
WHITE: THE KLAN

IN DECEMBER 1865, A GROUP of six bored young Confederate war veterans met in Pulaski, Tennessee, just north of the Alabama border. They decided to have some fun—to invent disguises, make up secret passwords, and call each other by odd names. Then they would gallop around town at night and engage in pranks. All six were college educated, and they named their group Kuklux, evidently from the Greek word "kuklos," which means "ring" or "circle." They might have known about a society in ancient Greece with a similar name that called itself "Circle of the Moon."

Their most obvious and appealing targets were local black residents. In one of the "pranks," a Kuklux member, dressed in a white sheet and a frightening mask, would ride up to the home of a black family after midnight and demand water. When given a well bucket, he would seem to drink it all down, but actually would be pouring the water into a rubber tube hidden beneath the sheet. Each time the bucket was empty, the man in the sheet would demand more. Eventually, the black man watching him would not be able to believe that anyone could drink so much. The man on the horse would thank his host, and say that he had not had a drink since he had been killed on the battlefield at Shiloh. The Kukluxer would then turn and gallop off into the darkness.

This sort of thing was good for a laugh, but soon the Kuklux members realized that many of the black men genuinely believed the ghosts of dead Confederate soldiers had risen in the night. They also realized that the terrified freedmen often thought the Kuklux were members of updated "slave patrols," which had ridden through the countryside at night before the Civil War, looking for runaways or any slaves who strayed out of their cabins without permission. Any poor wretch caught by these men would be brutally whipped or beaten.

When white supremacists understood the effect these strange "night riders" had on the black population, new groups popped up throughout the South. They called themselves "Klans," and it was not long before they began to use terror to "keep the freed slaves in line." "Insolence to former masters created a necessity for some kind of restraint, the whites believed. The Kuklux organization was designed to accomplish this purpose."

The Kuklux quickly began to function as a loose-knit

An engraving showing Kuklux Klansmen in North Carolina.

guerrilla army, whipping, beating, and sometimes killing black residents or burning their homes to the ground. Through terror and intimidation, the Klan in some areas operated as a shadow government, or, as some called it, "The Invisible Empire." But the Kuklux did not function simply to allow white supremacists to vent their anger. These groups had a definite agenda and at the center of it was preventing African Americans from voting.

It is difficult to appreciate just how much white Southerners

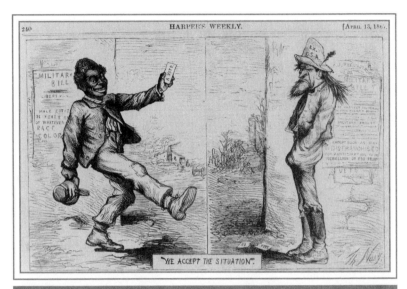

"WE ACCEPT THE SITUATION."

An 1867 political cartoon: A Confederate war veteran watches an African American vote.

hated the sight of African Americans casting ballots in free elections. Frank Alexander Montgomery, who had been a lieutenant colonel in the First Mississippi Cavalry, wrote that the Reconstruction Acts, by allowing freed slaves to vote, "filled to overflowing the cup of bitterness the south was called upon to drink." Montgomery, who would later serve both as a member of the Mississippi legislature and as a federal circuit court judge, thought it "impossible to conceive that the ingenuity of hate could have devised anything which would have so humiliated the white people of the state as this cruel and unnecessary act, by which the former slave was placed upon a political equality with his master, in many cases superior to his master, for often the slave could vote while the master could not . . . The negroes stood in a long line, patiently waiting each till his turn should come, and had no more idea what he was doing or who he was voting for than 'the man in the moon' had."

As always, Southerners thought themselves reasonable rather than bigoted. "The people of the north did not understand the character of the negro; to them, or the vast majority, he was a white man with a black skin, while we of the south knew him to be not only an alien race, but so vastly inferior that no fit comparison now occurs to me. Whatever traits of character he had which raised him from a condition of barbarism he owed to his association with the white man, and to-day it is well known that if he were even now removed from this association he would relapse into the lowest grade of humanity."

And so the Klan took specific aim at the Loyal Leagues. To white Southerners, these were "secret political organizations among the colored people, and were generally organized and presided over by their white allies. Meetings were usually held at night in some out-of-the-way place, and were harangued by white Republican speakers. These organizations solidified the black vote, for there was a league in every community, and every colored man was a member."

With the army concentrated in the cities or other densely populated areas, the Klan's reputation in the countryside as

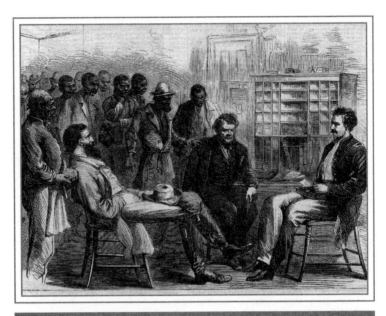

Loyal League meeting.

a terrorist organization beyond the reach of law spread dread among black residents. Often, Klan members needed simply to show up to keep black men from the voting booth. Even worse, in those cases, the Klan would not specifically have broken any laws.

"If a party of white men, with ropes conspicuous on their saddlebows, rode up to a polling place and announced that hanging would begin in fifteen minutes, though without any more definite reference to anybody, and a group of blacks who had assembled to vote heard the remark and promptly disappeared, votes were lost, but a conviction on a charge of intimidation was difficult. Or if an untraceable rumor that trouble was [looming] for blacks was followed by the mysterious appearance of horsemen on the roads at midnight, firing guns and yelling at nobody in particular, votes again were lost, but no crime or misdemeanor could be brought home to any one."

Even with the army in occupation, Klan terror was successful. In the presidential election of 1868, in eleven counties in Georgia, each with a majority of black voters, not a single vote was reported for Grant and the Republicans. That same year, when the Reconstruction state constitution was up for a vote in Mississippi, "it was charged by the Republicans . . . that whites terrorized the negroes by the Kuklux method, and either kept them away from the polls or intimidated them into voting against the Constitution."

By 1875, largely because of the campaign of terror by Klan groups and other violent white supremacist organizations, seven of the eleven secessionist states had been "Redeemed," or returned to Democratic control. The remaining four, Mississippi, Florida, Louisiana, and South Carolina, would become the centers of both the war-at-any-cost effort to restore white rule and the last desperate attempts to maintain at least some areas of equal rights in the South.

Perched on the fulcrum of this seesaw was the United States Supreme Court.

CHAPTER 6

TO THE COURT

DECIDING WHO SHOULD VOTE WAS not the only important question for which the delegates at the Constitutional Convention could not come up with a suitable answer. They also could not decide what the federal court system should look like or even, except for a Supreme Court, whether or not there should be one.

In 1787, most Americans did not want a federal court system at all, and certainly not one that had any real power. The new United States did not even have the money to pay a standing army, so siphoning off scarce funds to pay judges or build courthouses was considered a waste. But more important, most Americans thought of themselves as citizens of their home state first, and the United States second. Almost no one wanted to risk coming to trial in a court presided over by citizens of a different state, who they considered "foreigners." Many Americans were convinced a national court system would be an instrument of tyranny, claiming powers that were supposed to be reserved to their home state.

And so, Article III, which defined the federal court system, was kept short and vague. While there was mention of a "Supreme Court," there was no mention of how many judges would be on it. Nor did the delegates in Philadelphia fully define the Supreme Court's powers, how other courts would be organized, or whether they would exist at all. These questions were left to Congress to decide after the Constitution was in place.

Because distrust of a federal court system was so widespread, it became one of the topics most debated in the state conventions that were called to decide whether or not to ratify the new Constitution. Nine of the thirteen states would need to agree for the plan to be adopted. On June 21, 1788, New Hampshire became the ninth state to ratify, and so the Constitution was officially adopted. But neither Virginia nor New York had yet agreed, and many thought neither one would. Rejection in either state would be difficult for the new nation to overcome—rejection in both would likely destroy it.

In Virginia, the most important supporter was James Madison and the most vocal opponent the brilliant orator Patrick Henry. Henry, famed for proclaiming, "Give me liberty, or give me death," was also a fierce defender of slavery. He told his fellow Virginians that a national court system was a threat to their way of life. "They'll take your niggers

"GIVE ME LIBERTY, OR GIVE ME DEATH!"

PATRICK HENRY delivering his great speech on the Rights of the Colonies, before the Virginia Assembly, convened at Richmond, March 28th 1775. Concluding with the above sentiment, which became the war cry of the Revolution.

Patrick Henry proclaiming, "Give me liberty, or give me death!" His statements about black people are not as often quoted.

from you," he warned his fellow delegates in the convention Virginia had called to debate ratification. But Madison, also a slaveholder, was brilliant as well, and eventually, in a very close contest, Virginia agreed to ratify the Constitution.

In New York, where the opposition was even more intense, the battle for ratification was fought in part in New York City newspapers. An opponent of the Constitution who wrote under the name "Brutus" published a series of essays—similar to modern op-eds—in which he attacked the Constitution as a document that would surely lead to tyranny. Giving the central government so much power would trample on the rights of the people.

Brutus, whose identity remains unknown, was particularly critical of the new national court system, claiming it would be a tool with which the rich and powerful could oppress the ordinary citizen. About a Supreme Court whose members would never need to face an election and would serve for life, Brutus wrote, "There is no authority that can remove them, and they cannot be controlled by the laws of the legislature. In short, they are independent of the people, of the legislature, and of every power under heaven. Men placed in this situation will generally soon feel themselves independent of heaven itself." (There are many in the United States even today who share that view.)

Brutus seemed to be swaying New York against the Constitution, so in response, Alexander Hamilton, James Madison, and John Jay—writing jointly under the name "Publius"—published their own series of eighty-five essays in competing newspapers. These essays were later published together as *The Federalist* (generally known as *The Federalist Papers* today).

Essays on the new court system were penned by Hamilton, who insisted that federal courts would never be an instrument of tyranny. They would, in fact, be the "people's branch" of government. Judges, because they were independent, removed from the electoral process, would be in a position to protect ordinary citizens against any attempt at oppression by either Congress or the president.

Hamilton, as had Madison in Virginia, convinced the doubters, and New York ratified the new Constitution on July 26, 1788. But Hamilton's prediction about the weakness of the federal court system turned out to be wildly inaccurate. By the time the Reconstruction amendments came to be tested in the courts, the Supreme Court had acquired—or more aptly, seized—the authority to pass on any law as constitutional or not, and therefore whether it would remain in force or be struck down. (The 1803 case that established this power of "judicial review" was *Marbury v. Madison*, with the opinion written by Chief Justice John Marshall. It is usually the first case discussed in law school textbooks.)

The Fourteenth Amendment, written and enacted specifically to protect freed slaves, would prove to be especially fertile ground for the Court and began with an odd case and even odder participants.

CHAPTER 7

ANY WAY YOU SLICE IT: THE
SLAUGHTER-HOUSE CASES

THE FIRST TEST OF FOURTEENTH Amendment guarantees was brought to the Supreme Court not on *behalf* of black Americans, but rather *against* black Americans. The plaintiffs—the people suing—were a group of white New Orleans butchers whose practice of dumping foul, untreated, disease-ridden animal waste into the Mississippi River, just upriver from the pipes that supplied the city's drinking water, had caused a number of epidemics of cholera and yellow fever. The defendants were, in effect, the men of color who were members of the Louisiana state legislature and New Orleans city government.

White citizens of New Orleans had long hated the butchers, almost all of whom came from Gascony, a region in southwest France. In addition to sweeping the bones, organs, body parts, dung, and urine of cows, sheep, and pigs into the river, such that occasionally bits of these products would flow out of water taps, the Gascon butchers—notoriously independent, clannish, and hard-edged—had also conspired to keep the price of meat high. For years, New Orleans residents had pleaded with the governor and state and city legislators to *do something about it.*

Finally, in 1869, they did. Louisiana passed a law that required all butchers to slaughter, gut, and carve up animals in a single facility, downriver from the water supply and under the supervision of trained inspectors. This central slaughterhouse would be run by a corporation licensed by the state but owned by private individuals. Butchers would pay a small fee for every animal they acquired. Other cities, such as Boston and New York, had enacted similar laws and watched the rate of disease fall.

Although the butchers complained loudly that they were being denied the right to practice their trade as they wished, this law ordinarily would have evoked cheering from city residents. But it did not. That was because the legislature that passed the bill and the governor who signed it were Republicans, and, even worse, some of those legislators were black.

Democratic newspapers assailed the new law, accusing Republicans of setting up the central slaughterhouse not to protect the health of the citizenry, but to make money through corruption and graft. They also complained that the new facility would be available to anyone—which meant black butchers could use it as well.

New Orleans slaughterhouse.

With the encouragement of the same white supremacists who had been complaining about them for decades,
the butchers sued. They got nowhere in state courts—most
of the judges were Republican, and they drank city water—
so the butchers decided to try federal court. There, however,
they would need to find some way in which the new law violated their constitutional rights. So they claimed that forcing
them into a different place of business amounted to "involuntary servitude"—slavery—in violation of the Thirteenth
Amendment, and that the Fourteenth Amendment protected their "privileges and immunities" of citizenship, in

this case the right to conduct business how and where they wished.

Although the butchers' lawsuit seemed to rest only on how the language in the two amendments was interpreted, this case would actually become a chess match between two masterful adversaries, with language only the game pieces. Each knew his opponent well, and each loathed the other. One was an unapologetic white supremacist who had resigned a seat on the Supreme Court to become one of the leaders of the Confederacy; the other was a sitting justice who had been so opposed to slavery that he had left his native Kentucky in 1850 to move to free Iowa.

John A. Campbell.

Appearing for the butchers was John Archibald Campbell, who had joined the Supreme Court in 1853, after Chief Justice Roger B. Taney—the author of the notorious *Dred Scott* decision—and the other justices requested President Franklin Pierce appoint him. Campbell had been a legal prodigy, admitted to the bar in his native Georgia at age eighteen, so young that a special act of the state legislature had been required to allow him to practice. He left the Court in 1861, after his then home state of Alabama rejected the Union, and he was appointed assistant secretary of war by Confederate president Jefferson Davis. After Lincoln's assassination, Campbell had been arrested and held in jail for six months as a potential conspirator.

His opponent, Samuel Freeman Miller, was a no-nonsense, plain-speaking champion of equal rights. He had been born into a slaveholding family in Kentucky in 1816 but grew to detest slavery and those who practiced it. When he fled the South, he settled in Keokuk, Iowa, a Mississippi River port and a major shipping location for the same cattle, sheep, and hogs that in the 1860s would end up in New Orleans slaughterhouses.

Miller was more familiar with cholera than anyone in the courtroom—before entering the law, he had been a doctor who specialized in its treatment. That most physicians treated the disease as if it were still the

Samuel Freeman Miller.

Middle Ages, employing bleedings and purgatives, had infuriated him. Miller was convinced that cholera was transmitted
from unclean water, instead of "indigestible vegetables" or
"filthy and intemperate habits of the urban poor," but few
would listen to him. He finally abandoned medicine because
he could no longer bear to watch so much needless suffering
and death.

Almost immediately after entering the law, Miller had
gained a reputation for brilliance. He supported Abraham
Lincoln in the 1860 presidential election, and the new president rewarded him in 1862 with a nomination to the Supreme
Court. Miller was committed to racial equality and the goals
of Reconstruction, and he harbored a particular dislike for a
man he believed had dishonored the very court of which he
was now a member. He wrote to a friend that he "had never
seen nor heard of any action of Judge Campbell's since the
rebellion that was aimed at healing the breach he had contributed so much to make," and that Campbell was then merely "a
discontented and embittered old man."

Miller, therefore, heard the arguments in the *Slaughter-
House Cases* with a personal and scientific interest in proper
sanitation, a desire to support the biracial government of
Louisiana, and a deep distaste for John Campbell. While
none of these were supposed to affect Miller's judgment,

Campbell knew he had to find a way to turn those prejudices to his advantage.

In fact, John Campbell was a more complex figure than Miller gave him credit for. In his early career, and during his eight years on the Court, Campbell had been known as a master of compromise. Although he was in favor of slavery and believed in the superiority of the white race, he had advocated eventual emancipation and had even freed his own slaves before taking his seat on the Court. After the election of Abraham Lincoln, Campbell had tried to persuade the new president to negotiate on Southern secession. Lincoln refused, insisting that secession was against the law and no accommodation was possible. It was only then that Campbell returned home to take a position in the Confederate government. Even his imprisonment had been as a result of an effort to persuade Lincoln to soften his stance toward the defeated South.

But either his months in an army prison or what he saw as the injustice of Reconstruction had hardened him, and as the elevation of African Americans spread through Southern society, his every energy had come to be devoted to the return of white government.

Knowing how much Miller wanted to rule against him, Campbell set a trap. When the proposed Fourteenth Amendment was being debated in the House of Representatives,

John Bingham had made it clear that "privileges and immunities of citizenship" was meant to apply federal citizenship rights to the states. Bingham, of course, had been referring to the rights of newly freed slaves, who were guaranteed United States and state citizenship in the first sentence of the amendment.

But the amendment did not mention race, only "persons," and so Campbell insisted that it covered white citizens as well as black. Louisiana therefore had no right to herd butchers into a common facility and force them to pay fees to ply their trade. Unless, of course, state citizenship was different from national citizenship, with different "privileges and immunities." In that case, state governments could do things the federal government could not. Although Campbell carefully avoided saying so, if there were, in fact, two classes of citizenship, then states could pass other laws—about voting rights, for example—that fit their own definition.

Campbell had created an extremely clever argument. The Court could either support him and use the Fourteenth Amendment to protect a group of white, racist butchers who were poisoning New Orleans's drinking water, or they could rule against him and limit the amendment's reach by narrowing when its guarantees could be applied, especially for people of color. Although Campbell almost certainly did not inform his clients, his personal agenda of undermining

Reconstruction would have been much better served if he lost the case.

Which he did.

On April 14, 1873, by a 5–4 vote, the Court ruled that New Orleans had the right to require the butchers to relocate their business to a central location run by a corporation licensed for the task. "It is not true," Miller wrote for the majority, "that [this arrangement] deprives the butchers of the right to exercise their trade, or imposes upon them any restriction incompatible with its successful pursuit." (Miller also quickly dismissed the notion that requiring the butchers to relocate was "involuntary servitude," as defined by the Thirteenth Amendment.)

Miller made a point of lecturing Campbell on the meaning of the post-Civil War amendments. "An examination of the history of the causes which led to the adoption of those amendments and of the amendments themselves demonstrates that the main purpose of all . . . was the freedom of the African race, the security and perpetuation of that freedom, and their protection from the oppressions of the white men who had formerly held them in slavery." The Fourteenth Amendment, then, had not been enacted to shield white butchers from a state law meant to protect the health of its citizens.

But in his eagerness to destroy Campbell's argument, Miller had fallen into his trap. There was a "balance between

State and Federal power," Miller wrote, and those in the federal government "believed that the existence of the State with powers for domestic and local government, including the regulation of civil rights the rights of person and of property was essential to the perfect working of our complex form of government." So there was indeed a difference between citizenship in the United States and citizenship of a state, which meant that "privileges and immunities" might mean different things to each.

So, in overruling Campbell, Miller prevented the "privileges and immunities" clause of the Fourteenth Amendment from being used against state laws, which was exactly what Campbell had hoped he would do. Other rights that might be considered "privileges" of citizenship—like voting—could now be left almost solely to the whim of states. As a result of Miller's blunder, what should have been the strongest guarantee in the Fourteenth Amendment had become the weakest.

CHAPTER 8

INTERLUDE: PRECEDENT
AND POLITICS

A MERICAN LAW IS BASED ON a concept of "precedent." That means when a court decides a case, it is supposed to become a guide for judges in similar cases later, even those who may have disagreed with the decision. A precedent set by a lower court, however, is not binding on a higher court—the Supreme Court is free to overturn any decision it chooses. But once set, a Supreme Court precedent becomes mandatory for any other federal or state court to follow.

So, when Justice Miller wrote that the "privileges and immunities" clause of the Fourteenth Amendment did not apply to state governments, suddenly no court in America could use privileges and immunities to protect either African Americans or any other group of citizens whose rights had been trampled on. And, since decisions of the Supreme Court are also supposed to be binding on future Supreme Court decisions, that applied to future high court cases as well. Precedent, most legal scholars will insist, sets the rules for the future.

Except when it doesn't. In fact, Supreme Court history is filled with examples of the justices simply tossing aside a precedent, generally when the political climate either in the nation or on the Court has changed.

In 1896, for example, the Supreme Court, by an 8–1 majority, ruled in *Plessy v. Ferguson* that state laws imposing the forced separation of black people and white in railroad cars did not violate the Fourteenth Amendment as long as the facilities available to each race were "equal." "Laws permitting, and even requiring, their separation in places where they are liable to be brought into contact do not necessarily imply the inferiority of either race to the other," wrote Justice Henry Billings Brown for the majority. State legislatures, he added, were "at liberty to act with reference to the established usages, customs, and traditions of the people, and with a view to the promotion of their comfort and the preservation of the public peace and good order." This principle was soon applied across the South to theaters, schools, public toilets, cemeteries, and other facilities.

"Separate but equal," of course, was a sham even then, with black Americans forced into terribly substandard "colored only" facilities. Still, the precedent established in *Plessy* lasted until 1954, when the Supreme Court, in a unanimous decision in *Brown v. Board of Education*, ruled that separate but equal was "inherently *unequal*." "Does segregation of children in public schools solely on the basis of race, even though the physical facilities and other 'tangible' factors may be equal, deprive the children of the minority group of equal educational opportunities?" asked Chief Justice Earl Warren. "We believe that it does . . . We conclude that, in the field of public education, the doctrine of 'separate but equal' has no place."

And so the precedent that allowed legal segregation, at least in public schools, was tossed into the legal dustbin. Other decisions and acts of Congress followed so that, today, forced racial segregation "has no legal place" in any aspect of American life.

Another case involved whether or not the Second Amendment protects a private individual's right to own a gun. The amendment reads, "A well regulated Militia, being necessary to the security of a free State, the right of the people to keep and bear Arms, shall not be infringed." In 1938, Jack Miller, a bank robber, was charged with violating the 1934 National Firearms Act by transporting a sawed-off shotgun across state lines. He sued, claiming the law violated his Second Amendment rights.

In 1939, in a unanimous ruling, the Court ruled against Miller—who soon after was murdered by his associates for turning informer—saying "that a shotgun having a barrel less than 18 inches long [did not have] any reasonable relation to the preservation or efficiency of a well regulated militia," and such a weapon was not "any part of the ordinary military equipment, or that its use could contribute to the common defense." Therefore, the Second Amendment did not "guarantee to the citizen the right to keep and bear such a weapon."

The precedent that the Second Amendment applied only to "common defense" held until 2008, when, in *District of Columbia v. Heller*, the Court, in a 5–4 ruling, overturned both a Washington, DC, law that restricted gun ownership, even in private homes, and its previous ruling in *United States v. Miller*. Justice Antonin Scalia wrote the majority opinion. "The Second Amendment protects an individual right to possess a firearm unconnected with service in a militia, and to use that arm for traditionally lawful purposes, such as self-defense within the home," an interpretation that had been rejected by the Court in every previous case in which it had come under scrutiny. To support his opinion, Justice Scalia insisted that the first clause of the amendment, "A well regulated Militia, being necessary to the security of a free State," did not limit the second clause. The four dissenting justices, led by John Paul Stevens, called Justice Scalia's interpretation a "strained and unpersuasive reading."

Whether or not Justice Scalia or Justice Stevens was correct, the Court showed itself willing to reverse a ruling that the majority of justices came to disagree with. So, even though Justice Miller may have blundered by preventing the privileges and immunities clause of the Fourteenth Amendment from being used to protect the equal rights of black Americans—which included voting rights—the Court could easily have reversed itself.

But it never did. The precedent in the *Slaughter-House Cases* has held until this very day.

CHAPTER 9

EQUALITY BY LAW: THE CIVIL RIGHTS ACT OF 1875

ONCE BASIC GUARANTEES OF CITIZENSHIP had been secured for people of color, Radical Republicans planned to expand equal rights to everyday activities, such as eating in restaurants, going to the theater, or taking their families to public parks. By 1874, white America had lost any lingering desire to maintain a Reconstruction program. Keeping the army as an occupying force in the South was a huge drain on the nation's finances, and many thought that, by now, freedmen should be able to fend for themselves. In addition, most whites continued to think of people of color as members of an inferior race, perhaps a different species altogether. The Democratic Party played into these feelings. In the November 1874 congressional elections, they ran in both the North and the South on an anti-Reconstruction platform and made enormous gains in both houses.

As a result, when the new Congress was sworn in on

March 4, 1875, the House of Representatives would shift from a 199 to 88 Republican majority to a 182 to 103 edge for the Democrats. Since only a third of the Senate is up for reelection every two years, Republicans would keep control, but a 54–19 majority would shrink to 47–28. (One seat from Louisiana would remain vacant until January 1876, but that, too, would eventually be claimed by a Democrat.) At the next round of senatorial elections in November 1876, the Republican majority might easily disappear. President Grant would complete his second term in 1876 as well. While Grant was personally popular, many of the men he appointed had been accused, often accurately, of taking bribes or profiting from questionable deals. For the first time since before the Civil War, a Democrat was favored to win the presidency.

After the November 1874 disaster, Radical Republicans realized they had only four months to pass any further equal rights legislation. The problem was that many in their own party had no intention of voting for measures that would be unpopular with their constituents. In fact, to pass more equal rights legislation, moderate Republicans would be asked to vote *for* measures that they had voted *against* for years.

Back in 1870, Massachusetts senator Charles Sumner, one of the most ferocious proponents of racial rights, had proposed a bill in which the federal government would specifically guarantee "equal rights in railroads, steamboats, public conveyances,

Illustration depicts white people willing to be washed over a cliff rather than live cooperatively with people of color.

hotels, licensed theaters, houses of public entertainment, common schools and institutions of learning authorized by law, church institutions, and cemetery associations incorporated by national or State authority; also in jury duties, national and state." The notion of enforced integration in schools, churches, and cemeteries—in the North as well as the South—made most Republicans go pale. Sumner got nowhere.

Each year, Sumner had reintroduced his proposal, convinced that the Senate could not help but "crown and complete the great work of Reconstruction," but each year his party rejected it. Then, in March 1874, after a lifetime of trying to gain equality and justice for Americans of color, both slave and free, Charles Sumner died, his equal rights proposal seemingly dying with him.

But after the November 1874 elections, a strange thing happened. Championed by another Massachusetts congressman, Benjamin Butler—who had lost his own seat to a Democrat— Sumner's bill began to attract supporters. Many of them were Republicans who did not back Sumner in the past for fear of losing their seats, but who had now lost them anyway. Working tirelessly and overcoming a Democratic filibuster that reduced senators to "whiling away the hours by tearing newspapers to shreds [as] stale cigar smoke choked the air, and

Thomas Nast cartoon in *Harper's Weekly* celebrating the passage of the Civil Rights Act of 1875.

HAVE WHITE MEN ANY RIGHTS LEFT?

Senator Morrill, of Maine, who earnestly worked for the passage of the Civil Rights Bill, which gives to negroes the entrée of churches and schools, went into a colored people's church in Washington on Sunday night, and was told by one of the black dignitaries that the church was for colored persons, and that they wanted no white folks there. So he left.

Political cartoon protesting the Civil Rights Act of 1875.

members sprawled on the unswept carpet," Butler got Sumner's bill passed by both houses of Congress, although the schools, churches, and cemeteries provisions had to be dropped. On March 1, 1875, three days before the new Congress would take office, President Grant signed it into law.

Even with the omissions, "An act to protect all citizens in

the civil and legal rights," which became known as the Civil Rights Act of 1875, was an expansion of enforced equality that was awesome in its scope. Section 1 read, "All persons within the jurisdiction of the United States shall be entitled to the full and equal enjoyment of the accommodations, advantages, facilities, and privileges of inns, public conveyances on land or water, theaters, and other places of public amusement; subject only to the conditions and limitations established by law, and applicable alike to citizens of every race and color, regardless of any previous condition of servitude."

The law made violators liable for up to a $500 fine for each offense, payable to the person wronged, and, if convicted in criminal court, subject to a fine of between $500 and $1,000 and up to one year in jail. Section 3 gave federal, rather than state, courts jurisdiction over suits arising from the law and specifically granted federal officials powers of arrest over state officials who were in violation. Section 4 took aim at jury service and guaranteed that "no citizen possessing all other qualifications which are or may be prescribed by law shall be disqualified for service as grand or petit juror in court in the United States, or of any State, on account of race, color, or previous condition of servitude."

Passage of the Civil Rights Act evoked passionate response, although the direction of those passions was quite different depending on whom one asked. Black Americans rejoiced and moved immediately to exercise their new freedoms. Hoteliers, theater managers, restaurateurs, tavern owners, and railroad agents were suddenly swamped by requests for first-class tickets, dress circle theater seats, front tables, or a beer at the bar. Most white people, however, were equally determined to continue to exclude African Americans from public accommodations whenever they so chose. Across the Potomac from the nation's capital, the two principal hotels in Alexandria, Virginia, closed rather than let themselves be forced to rent rooms to people of color. (Both subsequently reopened when their owners realized that refusing blacks would not land them in any legal difficulty.) In Memphis, Tennessee, four African Americans demanded to be seated in the dress circle at a local theater. When the management grudgingly acceded, most of the white patrons walked out. In Richmond, Virginia, African Americans demanded service in restaurants, a tavern, and a barbershop, but in each case were refused.

Sentiment in the North was equally mixed. The *New York Times*, which had praised passage of the Fourteenth Amendment in 1868 as "settling the matter of suffrage in the Southern States beyond the power of the rebels to change it, even if they had control of the government," had a change of heart. "It has put us back in the art of governing men more than two hundred years," an editorial growled, "startling proof how far and fast we are wandering from the principles of 1787, once so loudly extolled and so fondly cherished."

Not every newspaper felt the need to be so outraged. The *Chicago Daily Tribune* quietly and correctly, as it turned out, predicted the law would have little real impact. "At present, its effect will be mainly political. It will be used on the one side to retain the hold of the Republican party on the negroes of the South; on the other, to excite new opposition to the Republican party among the whites." The writer added, "After the provision for enforced mixed schools had been eliminated from the bill, it became a comparatively insignificant measure."

Each newspaper accurately predicted where the fate of the law would be decided. The *Times*, with Confederacy-era sarcasm, said, "The Supreme Court, in instances such as this, is the last hope of all who attach any value to that somewhat despised instrument, the Constitution of the United States." The *Daily Tribune* agreed that the constitutionality of the bill would be settled in the Supreme Court and foresaw, again correctly, that the first challenges to enforcement would come from the North.

Most white businessmen and voting registrars simply ignored the law, and enforcement by other whites was minimal. Those denying black Americans their new rights of citizenship enjoyed the almost total support of police, politicians, and the courts. African Americans found themselves rarely successful in expanding their access to mainstream American life. A law on the books, they had learned, meant little if those to whom it was meant to apply refused to obey it, and authorities then refused to enforce it.

African Americans turned to the federal courts. A number of lawsuits were initiated in the hope that at least some judges would be unwilling to ignore a law whose provisions were so specific. In this, they were again mistaken. While in some rare instances the suits were successful, the vast majority were not. Some federal judges avoided the issue entirely, citing an impending decision by the Supreme Court, even though the justices had not yet agreed to hear an appeal of the law.

Nor would they for five years. Then they would take an additional three years to issue a ruling. But during that time, the Court would not be idle. In a series of decisions, it would lay the groundwork for taking back from black people almost every right of citizenship that the nation that had enslaved them had promised would be theirs.

CHAPTER 10

THE UNCERTAINTY OF LANGUAGE: *UNITED STATES V. REESE*

THE COURT BEGAN THAT PROCESS in April 1876, when it issued its first ruling that bore directly on the voting rights of African Americans.

In January 1873, William Garner, described by the Court as a "citizen of the United States of African descent," went to the tax collector in Lexington, Kentucky, to pay his poll tax of $1.50. Garner was employed, literate, and without a criminal record, and therefore could not be disqualified to vote in the state on any legal grounds. But the tax collector refused to take his money. Without a receipt for payment, Garner would be denied access to the ballot box in any election that year.

Tax collectors in Kentucky had come to regularly employ such a tactic to keep black men off the voting rolls. Garner next went to the office of the local election inspectors, Hiram Reese and Matthew Foushee, both white, and demanded a ballot for an upcoming municipal election.

Reese and Foushee refused, because, they said, Garner had failed to pay his poll tax. But Garner had come prepared and presented the two with an affidavit—a sworn statement—that he had attempted to pay the tax but had been turned away. The inspectors refused to accept the document.

That refusal just happened to be a specific violation of a federal law, the Enforcement Act of 1870, which said if an election official refused to allow any citizen to perform an "action required for voting," the citizen could present an affidavit that would qualify him. Garner filed a complaint with federal officials, stating that he had been illegally denied a constitutional right.

The Enforcement Act of 1870 had been the strongest effort to ensure the right to vote that the nation had ever undertaken. Expanding on the language of the Fifteenth Amendment, it mandated that any citizen of the United States must be allowed to vote in any election "in any State, Territory, district, county, city, parish, township, school district, municipality, or other territorial sub-division . . . without distinction of race, color, or previous condition of servitude." Further, it would be the duty of every person and officer in the electoral process "to give citizens of the United States the same and equal opportunity to . . . become qualified to vote without distinction of race, color, or previous condition of servitude." Anyone convicted of denying equal access to the ballot box—and the trial would be in federal, not state, court—would have to pay the person he wronged $500, and be liable for a jail term of up to one year. These penalties would apply to both Reese and Foushee.

Garner's appearance at the tax collector's and election office, as it turned out, had been a setup—what lawyers call a "test case"—part of a plan by Kentucky Republicans to ensure that black citizens were not turned away from the polls by white election officials. The local United States attorney, a lawyer working for the Department of Justice who prosecuted federal crimes—also a Republican—obtained a criminal indictment against Reese and Foushee, who would be forced to stand trial in Louisville.

United States v. Reese, as the case would be known, became as much a political fight as a legal one. Democrats grumbled that Reese and Foushee were being persecuted, "dragged all the way to Louisville at great expense to themselves and to the government to stand trial before strangers rather than their neighbors." Republicans countered that those "neighbors" would be all too happy to acquit two men who had blatantly broken the law in the name of white rule.

The trial was in United States circuit court and soon focused on just how much power the federal government had to define election standards for state and local governments. And that, in turn, became a question of language—just what, exactly, did the Fifteenth Amendment say after all? The circuit judges could not agree on specifics, so the case was referred to the Supreme Court.

Although the roster of associate justices on the Court was the same as for the *Slaughter-House Cases*, there had been a significant change at the top. The universally respected Chief Justice Salmon P. Chase had died and been replaced by Morrison R. Waite, a man who was viewed quite differently. In fact, never had a chief justice reached the Court as a lower choice of the president who nominated him and with less impressive credentials.

President Grant's first choice had not been one of the associate justices, each of whom wanted the job, but rather Senator Roscoe Conkling of New York, perhaps the most feared and powerful politician in the nation. But Conkling, known as the "king of partisanship," was hardly a legal scholar. His immense power in the Senate had come from trading favors and making secret deals with businessmen and other members of Congress, skills for which he had demonstrated a rare brilliance. Moving to the Supreme Court, even as chief justice, would vastly diminish his influence. Although few senators would have dared oppose him, to their great relief, he declined the appointment.

Grant then "stunned the nation" by nominating his attorney general, George H. Williams, widely considered a "legal

The "BOSS" PUZZLE

15—14—13.—THE GREAT PRESIDENTIAL PUZZLE.

Illustration showing Roscoe Conkling in 1880, trying to decide who should be president.

mediocrity" and "a weak if not corrupt politician who would have doubtless been hopeless as Chief Justice." Republican senators charged with confirming Williams's appointment were again in a difficult position. They did not want to openly oppose the head of their party, but nor did they want to vote for a man widely considered unqualified.

So they simply refused to act. They let the nomination linger in committee without taking a vote until a mortified Williams asked the president to withdraw his name. From there, the president tried seventy-three-year-old Caleb

Cushing, who had a long record of government service and had been attorney general under President Franklin Pierce. The Senate seemed willing to confirm him until an "anonymous source" reported that in 1861, Cushing had sent a very friendly letter to Jefferson Davis, president of the Confederate States of America, accepting the split in the Union as "accomplished fact." When Grant unearthed the letter and read it for himself, he immediately withdrew Cushing's nomination.

Having failed three times, Grant was determined that his next nominee would be confirmed. The only way to avoid the disasters that had befallen him to this point, Grant decided, was to choose someone no one in Washington had ever heard of. He found his man in Toledo, Ohio, a successful lawyer, well liked by all, but one who had never held a federal office or argued a case before the Supreme Court, or in Washington at all.

This was Morrison Waite. Waite found out he had been selected when a telegram arrived while he was having dinner. He was so surprised that he asked that the message be confirmed.

After Waite's nomination was announced and his record became public, the reaction was not favorable. Lincoln's secretary of the navy, Gideon Welles, remarked, "It is a wonder that Grant did not pick up some old acquaintance, who was a stage driver or bartender, for the place." The *Nation* added, "Mr. Waite stands in the front rank of second rank lawyers."

The *Chicago Daily Tribune* summed things up: "Although his practice has been extensive, he is not credited with the possession of more than a comfortable competence."

Despite what could generously be described as faint praise, Waite was unanimously confirmed and took his seat

Morrison R. Waite.

on March 4, 1874. Perhaps Congress was simply too fatigued to object. He was not greeted warmly by fellow justices. Not only had they been passed over for the seat Waite now held, but most of them regarded their new boss as an undeserving plodder. The only one of his colleagues who extended Waite any courtesy was Joseph Bradley, who invited the new chief justice and his wife to dinner their first night in the nation's capital. It was to be a friendship of enormous consequence for the nation.

Bradley, who had been on the Court since 1870, was everything Waite was not. He was considered one of the most technically proficient legal scholars ever to occupy a seat on the high bench, yet, where Waite was affable and social, Bradley was introverted and described himself as "cold and stoical." Other than mathematics and chess, he had almost no outside interests. He followed rigorous habits, rising, eating, working, and going to bed at precisely the same time every day. He was said to be "unconcerned with people, social life, or material rewards." When it came to the law, he was logical, thorough, and had total attention to detail.

Just weeks after Morrison Waite took his seat, Bradley had turned that logic, thoroughness, and attention to detail to the language of the Fifteenth Amendment, the very question that would lie at the core of *United States v. Reese.*

In those days, each Supreme Court justice also "rode circuit," that is, spent part of the year as a judge in United States circuit court in a specific part of the nation. Bradley's assigned territory included Louisiana, and there he sat in on an explosive case stemming from what would become known as the Colfax Massacre.

On Easter Sunday, April 13, 1873, upward of 150 heavily armed white men, most on horseback, some dragging a 4-pound cannon, converged on the courthouse of Colfax, seat of Grant Parish, in central Louisiana. In and around the courthouse were approximately 150 black defenders, also armed, but with antiquated, barely functioning shotguns, awaiting the invasion behind hastily constructed barricades. The confrontation had been precipitated by a disputed gubernatorial election in which both the Republican, a carpet-bagger, and the Democrat, a former Confederate officer, had been declared the winner. The issue was decided in the Republican-controlled courts with a predictable outcome.

After the white men besieged the courthouse, whether they offered terms of surrender was never totally clear. Once the shooting started, however, it became apparent that the out-gunned African American defenders had no chance. In short order, they gave up. After their weapons had been confiscated, the white invaders proceeded to slaughter their captives. As many as 100 black men were shot, stabbed, or burned to death in the courthouse. Afterward, the whites claimed the blacks had fired on them following the surrender, killing a Captain Hadnot, but that seemed unlikely since the bullet that had killed Hadnot had entered at an angle that could only have come from friendly fire.

Aware that Louisiana, even under a Republican governor, might not respond energetically to the killings, the federal government moved to charge members of the band for conspiracy under the very same Enforcement Act of 1870 that was used in *Reese*. In this case, the charges came under a part of the law that applied criminal penalties to activities that could be seen as interfering with the exercise of a person's constitutional rights.

Ninety-eight of the white invaders were charged with banding together with the intent of depriving the black men of their First Amendment right of free assembly. The white men could not be charged with murder, which was a state crime, and so they could not be tried for it in federal court. Only three men were convicted, and they appealed in circuit court, where Justice Bradley had decided to participate.

The three convicted murderers had based their appeal on the wording of the Fourteenth Amendment, which said no *state* could deprive any person of life, liberty, or property without due process of law, or deny any person equal protection of the laws. That meant, they claimed, that the amendment did not apply to the behavior of ordinary citizens, and that the Enforcement Act—which applied to individuals and not states—exceeded the federal government's authority. Controlling the behavior of individuals—prosecuting "ordinary crimes"—was solely the responsibility of state governments.

Justice Bradley's response would alter the course of American history.

There were occasions, Bradley wrote, in which the federal government could control the behavior of private citizens, but some very specific conditions had to be met. The only time the federal government could pass "positive laws" to protect individual rights was if that right did not exist before the Constitution defined it. The notion of "new rights" versus "old rights" was as confusing to most lawyers as to everyone else, so to illustrate his point, Bradley gave some examples.

One was the Fifteenth Amendment.

"The Fifteenth Amendment confers *no right to vote*," Bradley wrote. "That is the exclusive prerogative of the states. It does confer a right not to be excluded from voting by reason of race, color, or previous condition of servitude, and this is all the right that Congress can enforce."

Bradley's pivot on language totally changed both the amendment's meaning and its potential as a tool for the United States government to protect black voters. Under Bradley's definition, if an African American was threatened, beaten, and his house burned to the ground in order to terrorize him into not voting, and the state refused to prosecute the offenders, the federal government could do nothing, unless the victim could *prove* that the actions were motivated only by race—an almost impossibly high standard.

In this one opinion, Joseph Bradley had strangled the equal rights guarantees of not one but two constitutional amendments. He freed the three murderers, and the government announced that they would appeal to the Supreme Court. That case, *United States v. Cruikshank*, would be decided the same day as *United States v. Reese*. If Bradley's reasoning held up in the Supreme Court, it would establish precedent that all lower courts would be required to follow.

Which was precisely what occurred. Although Morrison Waite would write both opinions, each came from the cold, measured mind of Joseph Bradley.

In *Cruikshank*, Waite wrote, "The fourteenth amendment prohibits a State from depriving any person of life, liberty, or property, without due process of law; but this adds nothing to the rights of one citizen as against another." Waite added that the First Amendment right of assembly "was not intended to limit the powers of the State governments in respect to their own citizens, but to operate upon the National Government alone." As a result, "for their protection in its enjoyment . . . the people must look to the States. The power for that purpose was originally placed there, and it has never been surrendered to the United States." So despite what the drafters of the amendment had intended and those ratifying the amendment thought they were agreeing to, the Bill of Rights applied to the federal government only, not the states.

In *Reese*, Waite lifted Bradley's language almost verbatim. "The Fifteenth Amendment to the Constitution does not confer the right of suffrage, but it invests citizens of the United States with the right of exemption from discrimination in the exercise of the elective franchise on account of their race, color, or previous condition of servitude, and empowers Congress to enforce that right by 'appropriate legislation.'" From there, the question became what Congress may or may not do to enforce the amendment. "The power of Congress to legislate at all upon the subject of voting at state elections rests upon this amendment, and can be exercised by providing a punishment only when the wrongful refusal to receive the vote of a qualified elector at such elections is because of his race, color, or previous condition of servitude." And because the third and fourth sections of the Enforcement Act of 1870 were not "confined in their operation to unlawful discrimination on account of race, color, or previous condition of servitude," they were "beyond the limit of the Fifteenth Amendment and unauthorized."

As a result of these two decisions, March 27, 1876, when they were handed down, can well be considered the day that Joseph Bradley and Morrison Waite began the process that would return black American citizens to slavery in all but name. But the road map for the return to white supremacy in the United States still needed to be more specifically laid out, which the Court would proceed to do over the next twenty-seven years.

CHAPTER 11

RUTHERFRAUD ASCENDS, BUT NOT EQUAL RIGHTS

To THE SURPRISE OF BOTH his supporters and detractors, Ulysses Grant decided not to run for a third term in 1876. The ongoing scandals that plagued his administration played a big role in his decision, as did the tradition, begun by George Washington, of leaving office after two terms.

In Grant's place, Republicans nominated Rutherford B. Hayes, a former Union army general who after the war became a congressman and then a "reform" governor of Ohio. Democrats chose a reformer of their own, Governor Samuel Tilden of New York, who had successfully attacked the almost impossibly corrupt Tammany Hall political machine run by William Magear "Boss" Tweed.

Hayes ran as all Republicans had, as a friend to black Americans. He felt he had little choice. Without the black vote in the South, he appeared to have no chance of being elected. But while Hayes was pledging to maintain the social advances of Reconstruction, Tilden aimed his appeal at "white Southerners who sought to recapture the control of their state governments from Republican carpetbaggers and from newly free African Americans." If Tilden were elected, white Southerners knew, he would surely withdraw the army from the South.

When the ballots were counted, Tilden had won the popular vote easily and could solidly claim 184 electoral votes, one short of the number needed for election. Hayes could claim only 165. Twenty electoral votes had yet to be assigned, nineteen of which were in Florida, Louisiana, and South Carolina, each of which was still under Republican control. Still, Tilden was generally assumed to have won each of the three, since, in what originally seemed a surprise, he had won every other state in the South. (Hayes had won in the Midwest and West, and so the contested electoral vote in Oregon was almost certain to be his.)

But soon reports began to drift in that throughout the South, black voters had been intimidated, brutalized, or denied the right to vote. Fraud had been everywhere, with ballot boxes stuffed with nonexistent Democratic votes, or Republican votes destroyed. Still, no matter how he achieved it, if even one of these disputed electoral votes went to Tilden—and just by the count, he certainly seemed entitled to some of them—he would be the new president.

Almost every newspaper in America reported Tilden as

the winner. The *New York Times*, however, which on the day before the election had proclaimed, "Republican Success Certain," the day after the election ran the headline "Result Still Uncertain." During the Civil War, the *Times*'s managing editor, John C. Reid, had been held as a prisoner at the Confederacy's infamous Andersonville prison and despised Democrats. On election night, Reid convinced local Republican leaders to contest the election even though Tilden seemed to have won. The New Yorkers telegraphed fellow Republicans, telling them to dispute the results in any Southern state where Tilden's victory might be overturned. Official challenges were filed in Louisiana, Florida, and South Carolina.

The next day, the *New York Times* reported, "The Battle Won. Governor Hayes Elected—The Republicans Carry Twenty-one States, Casting 185 Electoral Votes." To get to 185, the *Times* had awarded all three states' electors to Hayes. The article claimed to be based on canvasses—examinations of the votes—although the *Times* was vague on just who had done the canvassing.

Canvassing boards were indeed appointed in each state by the sitting Republican governments, although not until after the *Times* ran its piece. Not surprisingly, each state confirmed what the *Times* had reported and declared Hayes the winner.

Democrats were furious. The party that was all too happy

to win as a result of fraud felt differently about losing because of it. Very real threats of armed revolt spread throughout Washington. Militias were raised in the countryside and calls for secession were heard for the first time since the war. A shot was fired at Hayes's home

Rutherford B. Hayes.

in Ohio while the candidate was having dinner inside.

Nothing in the Constitution or federal law discussed what to do in such a situation, but both sides knew they had to do something. Eventually, they decided to appoint a fifteen-man Electoral Commission—five senators, five representatives, and five Supreme Court justices. Fourteen would be members of the two parties, divided equally, and the fifteenth, someone both sides agreed would judge the issue on its merits only. Almost certainly, this meant that *one man* would choose the next president of the United States. Anyone who had previously voiced even a whisper of preference for the Democrats or the Republicans would be unacceptable to the other party. With both sides ready almost to go to war, many doubted that such a man even existed.

But incredibly, that man *did* seem to exist and, even better, be available. He was Associate Justice David Davis. A Lincoln appointee, he was so trusted as an independent that it was said, "No one, perhaps not even Davis himself, knew which presidential candidate he preferred."

But after Davis had been named, Democrats decided they were not all *that* comfortable with the Republican-appointed justice, so they thought to shift the odds a bit. Before the commission could meet, the Democratic-controlled state legislature in Illinois offered Davis a vacant seat in the United States Senate. Republican newspapers denounced this transparent attempt to butter up the swing vote. Both sides assumed Davis would decline the seat and remain on the Court, but that the honor of being named senator just might help tip his vote toward Tilden.

But then, confounding everyone, Davis accepted. He resigned his seat on the Court to be senator from Illinois. He never said why, but he clearly did not want the responsibility of selecting a president by himself.

Since four of the justices were already on the commission, one of the remaining four would be forced to take Davis's place. Each was closely associated with one of the political parties. For reasons never made public, Joseph Bradley was the man chosen. Democrats denounced the choice as a fix, but after the Davis fiasco, their credibility was somewhat strained.

Bradley, who did not share Davis's hesitancy, accepted the appointment and thus became the only man in American history empowered to choose a president essentially on his own.

Bradley, always careful and meticulous, and proud of both his objectivity and his intellect, drew up a detailed written opinion for each man. But Joseph Bradley was one of those people who, after careful consideration of the facts, always seemed to come down on the side of a question that matched the beliefs he had held going in. And so it was here. Bradley chose Hayes.

Democrats' fury was renewed. Some once more threatened rebellion. Rumors circulated that an army of 100,000 men was prepared to march on the capital to prevent "Rutherfraud" or "His Fraudulency" from being sworn in. In the House of Representatives, Democrats began a filibuster to prevent Hayes's inauguration.

What happened next has been a subject of debate among historians ever since. The most widely accepted version is the simplest and the most likely. "Reasonable men in both parties struck a bargain at Wormley's Hotel. There, in the traditional smoke-filled room, emissaries of Hayes agreed to abandon the Republican state governments in Louisiana and South Carolina while Southern Democrats agreed to abandon the filibuster and thus trade off the presidency in exchange for the end of Reconstruction." The "Compromise of 1877," as it

THE POLIT

18

We can prove beyond a shadow of doubt that Louisiana and Florida voted for TILDEN by decisive majorities, and we are prepared to show up the villainous frauds of the Returning Boards. All we ask is investigation by this commission.

Clifford, Field, Bayard, Abbott, Hunton, Thurman & Payne.

We would be perfectly willing to examine into the merits of the case, but the evidence is all against us. We therefore declare it "Aliunde," 7 into 8 once, and "Joe Bradley" over.

Miller, Strong, Morton, Garfield, Frelinghuysen, Edmunds, Hoar & Bradley.

FREDERICK T. FRELINGHUYSEN

GEORGE F. EDMUNDS

KENNER

CASE

LOUISIANA

SAMUEL F. MILLER

THE TWO NEGROE

Who defeated the will of the America
on the 7th da

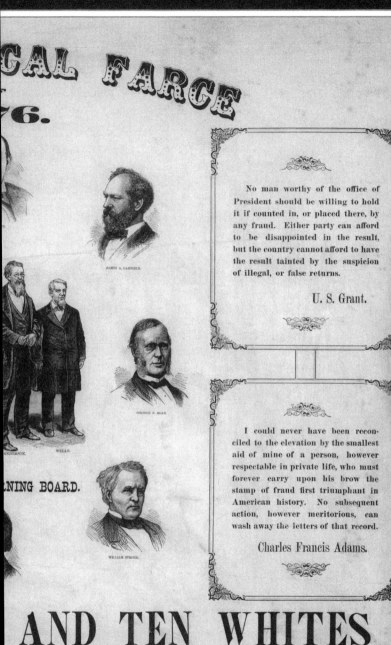

GAL FARCE
6.

JAMES A. GARFIELD.

ANDERSON.   WELLS.

NING BOARD.

GEORGE F. HOAR.

WILLIAM STRONG.

No man worthy of the office of President should be willing to hold it if counted in, or placed there, by any fraud. Either party can afford to be disappointed in the result, but the country cannot afford to have the result tainted by the suspicion of illegal, or false returns.

U. S. Grant.

I could never have been reconciled to the elevation by the smallest aid of mine of a person, however respectable in private life, who must forever carry upon his brow the stamp of fraud first triumphant in American history. No subsequent action, however meritorious, can wash away the letters of that record.

Charles Francis Adams.

AND TEN WHITES

e, as expressed through the Ballot box,
ovember 1876.

Entered, according to act of Congress, in the year 1877, by JOSEPH A. STOLL, in the office of the Librarian of Congress at Washington.

A560010

A Democratic Party poster calling the election of 1876 a fraud.

SHALL WE CALL HOME OUR TROOPS?

We intend to beat the Negro in the battle of life, and defeat means one thing—EXTERMINATION."—*Birmingham (Alabama) News*

Republican cartoon predicting disaster for African Americans if the army is withdrawn from the South.

came to be known, made Rutherford B. Hayes the nineteenth president of the United States. As one of his first orders of business, the man who had run for president promising to defend the civil rights of black Americans ordered federal troops withdrawn from the South. Without the army to enforce fair voting, the intimidation, murder, and fraud that had come to characterize Southern elections could proceed undeterred.

And so, when the soldiers marched out, they took Reconstruction with them.

CHAPTER 12

THE COURT GIVETH . . . :
STRAUDER V. WEST
VIRGINIA

THAT LEFT THE SUPREME COURT as the one institu-
tion of government that could determine what the
Constitution required in terms of voting rights for American
citizens of color. On March 1, 1880, in rulings on the appeals
of two quirky murder convictions, the Court began to do so.
The first involved the long, unlikely road to justice for an
African American confessed ax murderer.

On Friday, April 19, 1872, the headline in the Wheeling,
West Virginia, *Daily Intelligencer* read, "Horrible Murder. A
Colored Woman Tomahawked by Her Husband. He Brains
Her with a Hatchet. The Murderer Escapes." The article
detailed how Taylor Strauder, a local carpenter, had savagely
murdered the woman he had wed only months before.
Strauder, an extremely jealous man, had made the mistake of
marrying a woman who had been constantly unfaithful. He

had been out drinking the night before the murder, and when he arrived home, he heard the back door of the cottage in which he lived slam shut as he was entering through the front. He accused his wife of entertaining other men, and the two fought nearly all night. Early the following morning, the fight resumed. Finally, rather than continue to deny her husband's accusations, she allegedly turned to him from her rocking chair and said, "What are you going to do about it?" Moments later, the hatchet fell across Mrs. Strauder's skull.

A few days later, Strauder was apprehended in Pittsburgh. He was returned to Wheeling, jailed, assigned a lawyer, and left for what everyone expected to be a brief wait until he was tried and hanged. But what neither Taylor Strauder nor anyone else involved in this case could have known was that Mrs. Strauder's murder would not only set in motion an incredible three-decade odyssey for the accused, but it also set the scene for one of the most celebrated voting rights cases in American history.

Strauder proved to be a cooperative and amiable prisoner, popular with both the guards and the other inmates. As a result, the authorities did not rush to bring him to trial, content to let him remain in jail rather than hang. But West Virginia had a law stating that anyone accused of a crime who remained in prison without trial for three sessions of the circuit court would go free. It was not until the third of these, in May 1873, that Strauder was actually brought before a judge.

His lawyer was thirty-one-year-old Blackburn B. Dovener, a staunch Republican who had left his native Virginia to fight for the Union. He had entered the army as a private, raised a company of soldiers while still a teenager, and, during the conflict, been promoted to captain. After his discharge, he turned to the law.

Before Strauder could come to trial, Dovener made a motion to remove the case to federal court on constitutional grounds. In March 1873, West Virginia had passed a law that stated, "All white male persons who are twenty-one years of

Blackburn Dovener.

age and who are citizens of this State shall be liable to serve as jurors, except as herein provided." Dovener argued that restricting the jury to whites only violated the equal protection clause of the Fourteenth Amendment. His motion was denied.

On May 9, 1873, Taylor Strauder was found guilty of first-degree murder in state court and sentenced to be hanged. Two weeks later, Dovener was back in court, submitting motions to gain Strauder a new trial. The motions were denied, and Strauder was given an August 29, 1873, date for his execution. Dovener once again announced his intention to appeal.

But Strauder himself remained in the news, and the tone of the reporting began to change. In July 1873, he was reported to have undergone a spiritual conversion. "The pastor of the 5th Street African Methodist Church and several of the members of that congregation visited the jail on Sunday evening and administered the rite of baptism," newspapers reported. "Afterwards they engaged in devotional services . . . Jailer Kennedy informs us that the condemned man deeply feels his position and that Strauder is misunderstood."

Strauder had also come to be on such good terms with his jailers and local deputies that they openly advocated that the man who had cleaved in his wife's skull with a hatchet be allowed to live. Two weeks before his execution date, Dovener succeeded in persuading the state supreme court to put off the execution until his motions could be ruled on. On August 29, a newspaper ran a small item about the execution under the heading "Not today."

In January 1874, with Taylor Strauder now seemingly a permanent tenant of the county jail, the state supreme court put the matter off until July. Then, in what was a surprise to everyone, none more so than to Strauder himself, the supreme court ordered a new trial. They did so not on constitutional grounds, but rather due to an error by the prosecutors in filing the charges. On November 5, 1874, Strauder was once again convicted of first-degree murder and sentenced to hang, and just as quickly, Blackburn Dovener was back in court, petitioning.

In January 1875, that petition was denied and Strauder was again given a date of execution, this time March 26. He took the news placidly, as always, and was the object of great sympathy from jail personnel with whom he had by then been associated for almost three years. In early March, one newspaper reported bets were being taken on whether or not the sentence would be carried out. Sure enough, the very next week, a state supreme court judge granted a stay of execution, pending a decision on appeals by the defendant.

From there, the appeals went back and forth for almost two years. All the while, Taylor Strauder remained in county jail, not free, but not especially restrained either. Three days before Christmas 1876, the Ohio County commissioners made their annual inspection of the jail, accompanied by reporters. As they opened the door, "Immediately a colored man came out of one of the cells to the left and approached the barred door. The turnkey handed him a key, which he took and proceeded to lock up in their cells the prisoners who were sauntering idly about taking their regular afternoon exercise. The prisoners all safely in their cells, the colored man returned to the door and handed back the key.

"The colored man," the reporter observed, "was no other than Taylor Strauder, the noted wife murderer, [who] appeared to be well acquainted with the party, and a great favorite as well, as he shook hands cordially all around and conversed freely with them."

Strauder had also taught himself to read and write and mentioned that he intended to write a book about his experience as a prisoner.

In November 1877, when the state supreme court again denied Dovener's motion that the trial be moved to federal court due to discrimination in jury selection, he applied to remove the case to the United States Supreme Court on Fourteenth Amendment grounds. On April 15, 1878, Chief Justice Waite announced that the Supreme Court would hear the appeal. Ten days later, Taylor Strauder marked his sixth anniversary as a prisoner in the county jail, the longest any inmate had ever been held in that facility.

Strauder v. West Virginia was not heard until October 1879, but it was billed as one of the most important cases regarding African American civil rights ever heard by the Supreme Court. To add to the drama, United States Attorney General Charles Devens, a former Union army general who served with

Ulysses Grant, had joined the Strauder legal team, and Senator John Brown Gordon of Georgia, a former Confederate general who served with Robert E. Lee, worked with the state.

On March 1, 1880, the Court finally rendered its verdict. By a 7–2 vote, the justices ruled that Strauder's conviction would be overturned because he had been deprived of equal protection of the laws as guaranteed to him under the Fourteenth Amendment.

Justice William Strong, an abolitionist from Connecticut, wrote the opinion. He said that the case was "not whether a colored man . . . has a *right* to a grand or a petit jury composed in whole or in part of persons of his own race or color, but it is whether . . . all persons of his race or color may be excluded by law *solely* because of their race or color." He echoed Justice Miller in pointing out the reason the Fourteenth Amendment was adopted, "securing to a race recently emancipated, a race that, through many generations, had been held in slavery, all the civil rights that the superior race enjoy."

Strong did, however, make certain these lofty sentiments were kept in their proper context. "The colored race, as a race, was abject and ignorant, and in that condition was unfitted to command the respect of those who had superior intelligence. Their training had left them mere children, and, as such, they needed the protection which a wise government extends to those who are unable to protect themselves."

Nonetheless, the West Virginia statute limiting jury participation to white men could not be justified, even if the aim was merely to ensure that "abject and ignorant children" did not sit in judgment on more qualified members of society. "The very fact that colored people are singled out and expressly denied by a statute all right to participate in the administration of the law as jurors because of their color, though they are citizens and may be in other respects fully qualified, is practically a brand upon them affixed by the law, an assertion of their inferiority, and a stimulant to that race prejudice which is an impediment to securing to individuals of the race that equal justice which the law aims to secure to all others."

With Strauder's conviction overturned eight years after his initial arrest, West Virginia officials were left with the question of what to do with him. Even if the state did opt for a retrial, the case had to clear hurdles in federal circuit court, where Dovener moved to have Strauder released, or at least freed on bail while Ohio County officials decided whether to retry him. That process dragged on for a year, until finally, on April 30, 1881, Judge J. J. Jackson ordered Strauder freed. But even that did not end the matter. As he walked out of the courtroom, he was once again arrested. West Virginia had decided to try him again after all.

Strauder's reaction was hardly one of surprise. As he stepped off the train with his captor, "looking very well . . . dressed neatly and tastefully," he said, "Yes sir, I am here again, and under arrest, but this don't amount to anything. There wasn't any use in arresting me no how, as I intended to come right here as soon as ever I got free. Did it surprise me any? Not a bit. I 'spected it all the time. I knew of the intention of the parties here shortly after they made the move. Do I feel uneasy? Not a bit. The trouble has all been gone over once, and I don't think I should have to use the same gauntlet again. I feel sure that I shall be free in a few days."

And so he was. Three days later, he was taken before a justice of the peace and discharged.

The following year, Strauder got married again, this time to Minnie Johnson, a woman, possibly white, he had met while he was in jail. Minnie Johnson died three years after that, however—of natural causes—while Strauder seemed to have been away, on the job as a riverboat carpenter. Taylor Strauder then slipped from public view.

For Blackburn Dovener, it was the reverse. Regardless of where one stood on the particulars of the case, *Strauder v. West Virginia* was a legal triumph, and Dovener became one of his state's most sought-after attorneys. Just two years after he secured Strauder's final release, Dovener was elected to the

West Virginia state legislature, and in 1894, to Congress, representing West Virginia's First District.

But Dovener was not yet through with Taylor Strauder. In April 1898, with Dovener now a respected national figure, his erstwhile client was back in the news.

"Taylor Strauder, known as Andrew E. Strauder, shot and probably fatally wounded Ida Houston, his white sister-in-law, tonight. She in turn shot him in the forehead, neck and shoulder, and he may die. Strauder was separated from his wife, Katherine Strauder, a few months ago, she refusing to live with him when she heard he had murdered his first wife in Wheeling. He demanded admittance to her home, at 5 Arthur Street tonight, was refused and then forced the door in. He fired two shots at Mrs. Strauder, neither taking effect and the Houston woman then rushed to a trunk and secured a revolver. Just as she was about to fire, Strauder fired three times at her, one bullet entering the abdomen. The wounded woman emptied her revolver at Strauder, three shots taking effect. The life of the woman is almost despaired of, and physicians fear Strauder's wounds will end in death." The article also noted that Strauder, who had actually been married three times, was an extremely jealous man who suspected his wife of infidelity.

Word of Strauder's arrest and imminent death rekindled

interest in his earlier trials. Dovener, by now reluctant for the public to be reminded that, because of his efforts, a murderer had gone free, granted an exclusive interview with the *Wheeling Daily Intelligencer*, in which he attempted to put the best possible face on the affair. He concluded, "As a result of this long fight against the discrimination on colored men, the legislature of our state amended the jury law by striking out the word 'white,' and it, as amended, remains the law today."

In a final irony, Strauder did not die of his wounds, nor did Ida Houston. He was arrested, tried, and convicted of attempted murder, and sentenced to prison. It was only then that Taylor Strauder disappeared permanently into history. Already in his sixties, he most likely died in jail, but there is no record of when or where it occurred, or where Strauder's final remains are buried.

After twelve years in Congress, Blackburn Dovener was defeated for renomination in 1906. He lived for eight more years until his death at age seventy-two and was buried in Arlington National Cemetery.

CHAPTER 13

. . . AND THE COURT
TAKETH AWAY:
VIRGINIA V. RIVES

WHEN HIS CONVICTION WAS OVERTURNED, Taylor Strauder might have become known, at least indirectly, as the man who secured voting rights for black Americans. But what the Supreme Court granted, it could just as easily nullify, which it did, not two hours later, in a case every bit as odd and unusual as that of the West Virginia ax murderer.

It all started when a white teenager yelled "school-butter."

Although the term sounds silly today, in the 1870s, it seems, it was a most extreme insult. "To any who have known the conditions existing in backwoods schools it is unnecessary to explain this phrase," a Kentucky man wrote. "What it originally meant, if indeed it meant anything, the writer has never been able to learn, nor to obtain a reasonable explanation. But from rural Pennsylvania to Arkansas, and even in parts of Indiana and Michigan, it was known as the most humiliating insult, and one certain to provoke swift revenge. All rules against fighting stood aside in favor of a pursuit of the person who called the word to the school."

In mid-November 1877, twenty-two-year-old Aaron Shelton's younger brother, likely about sixteen, yelled "school-butter" as he was passing an African American school in Patrick County, Virginia. Patrick County is in the eastern part of the state, on the border of North Carolina. Along with Henry County, immediately to the east, it was named in honor of the famous Virginia patriot and orator, who also happened to be one of the state's most fervent defenders of slavery.

What happened next was not totally clear. The younger Shelton told his brother that some of the students at the school, including eighteen-year-old Lee Reynolds, gave him a "ducking," which usually meant pushing him underwater, although this incident might have involved simply pouring water on his head. Lee Reynolds's brother Burwell, who was nineteen, was also said to be a participant in the ducking.

About two weeks later, on November 27, Aaron Shelton, who was "of extraordinary physical development," was passing the school to fetch a load of logs for his uncle's sawmill and he yelled "school-butter," without provoking a response. Later that day, however, during recess, in which the teacher had "left his school in charge of one of the grown and advanced scholars," another of Aaron Shelton's brothers, this one only thirteen, yelled "school-butter" at those playing outside. They chased him and he ran to where his brother was loading his wagon.

That provoked a confrontation in which Aaron Shelton told the black children that he would yell "school-butter" whenever he wanted, and that if anyone objected, "he would shoot their heart-strings out." If the teacher interrupted, he would shoot him as well. One of the black children was the Reynolds brothers' younger sister, to whom Shelton used "abusive language." That evening, "Shelton and the Reynolds boys had a dispute about some logs Shelton's uncle had cut and left in the road."

The stage was then set for the final confrontation between Aaron Shelton and the Reynolds brothers. It took place on November 29, 1877, when Shelton was hauling a wagon up the road to pick up the load of logs. Lee and Burwell Reynolds were leading their father's team of horses in the opposite direction on the same road. A quarrel ensued. According to one of Shelton's younger brothers, Green, who was a witness to the events, the confrontation quickly escalated and Lee Reynolds took a shot at Shelton with the rifle he always carried. The shot missed and Shelton, wielding a heavy stick, charged Lee Reynolds and knocked him to the ground. "At that time, Burwell Reynolds ran up and stabbed Shelton in the back with a large butcher knife." Aaron Shelton died on the spot.

Lee Reynolds was arrested at the scene. His brother fled the county but was soon caught. Each claimed that Green Shelton's version of the events was a lie: No gun was ever fired; Aaron Shelton started the fight by charging at Lee with a length of lumber; the knife had been Shelton's; he died after being stabbed in the struggle he began; Burwell Reynolds had merely tried to separate the two, as Shelton was much stronger than Lee.

Perhaps not surprisingly, which version residents of Patrick County believed was determined almost solely by race. Since the grand jury that was to decide whether or not to bring criminal charges was all white, both brothers were indicted for first-degree murder, the most serious offense possible. For Lee Reynolds, in particular, the charge was extreme because he had not personally had a hand in Aaron Shelton's killing.

The Reynolds's lawyers were white, and, like Blackburn Dovener, war veterans. This time, however, the two men— Colonel William Martin and Captain A. M. Lybrock—had fought for the Confederacy. Martin, in his sixties, had a long record of public service, and, "as a lawyer, orator, and statesman, he was regarded as the peer of any man in Virginia." He had lost a brother in the war. Although they had fought to defend slavery, they would defend the Reynolds brothers with as much energy as if they had been white.

Their first problem was in jury selection. Virginia law stated, "All male citizens twenty-one years of age, and not over sixty, who are entitled to vote and hold office, under the constitution and laws of this state, shall be liable to serve as jurors." In practice, however, a trial judge picked a pool of potential jurors as he wished, and then placed their names in a box from which the actual trial jurors were selected. For this trial, as for just about every trial in Virginia, the judge chose a jury pool that was exclusively white. Martin and Lybrock petitioned the judge to include men of color, since the verdict of an all-white jury was almost certain to be unfavorable to the defendants. The judge refused, replying that he had chosen the jury pool according to law. That no black men were included—or were ever included in Patrick County—was not an issue for the court.

Martin and Lybrock then asked that the trial be moved to federal court on constitutional grounds. The judge refused. Lee and Burwell Reynolds chose to be tried separately and each was found guilty, Burwell of first-degree murder, Lee of second. On technical grounds, Martin and Lybrock managed to get a new trial for each. Their motion to have the retrial moved to federal court was denied.

Lee was again found guilty and sentenced to eighteen years in prison. Martin and Lybrock, however, succeeded in obtaining a hung jury—one in which the vote was not unanimous—for Burwell on the grounds that first-degree murder, which required that Burwell had decided in advance to kill Shelton, had not been proven. That Burwell would be convicted of second-degree murder, like his brother, there was no doubt. At that point, Martin and Lybrock filed a motion with United States District Court Judge Alexander Rives to have both cases heard in federal court.

They could not have made a better choice.

Bright, quirky, and fearless, Rives had spent his entire adult life following his own dictates with little or no concern for the opinions or even the loathing of friends, family, neighbors, or peers. Both his mother—a Cabell—and his father were members of the "First Families of Virginia," with a long tradition of gracious living, deference to authority, and slave owning. From an early age, Rives not only demonstrated a dislike of all three, but made it quite clear that he would live his life as he pleased. He put them on notice just after his twentieth birthday, when, rather than taking a bride from Virginia gentry, he chose a minister's daughter, two years his senior and an immigrant besides. The two would remain married until her death in 1861 and have ten children. (Rives took a new wife the very next year.)

After Hampden-Sydney College, in which he enrolled at age fifteen, Rives studied law at the University of Virginia. Upon graduation, he accepted a professorship at a small Virginia college, resigned it soon afterward, and returned to Charlottesville to start a law practice. For a time, he handled mostly real estate transactions, but in 1845, he leapt into the public eye under extremely peculiar circumstances.

When officials at the University of Virginia had attempted to crack down on a series of pranks by a group of students who called themselves "Calathumpians," disturbances had erupted that escalated into full-blown riots. The Calathumpians had formed the year before and were composed of "exemplary students bent on 'fun, frolic, and childish folly.'" With alcohol as a contributing agent, the students soon began to engage in behavior that their elders did not deem childish folly at all. When three Calathumpians were suspended in February 1845 for "raising a scene of disorder at one of the college hotels"—dormitories—the others in the group put on masks and "made an attack with sticks and stones on the home of the chairman."

A truce was arranged and held for about six weeks. In April, Calathumpians surrounded the home of an unpopular professor, raised a din with horns and drums, and soon afterward began pounding on his windows, terrifying his wife. They dispersed only when the professor appeared with a rifle and promised to shoot anyone who refused to leave. The

Calathumpians retreated but were soon laying siege to the homes of university officials across the campus. Windows were broken, and even the famed university rotunda, designed by Thomas Jefferson, was pitted with damage from stones.

University officials began to consider calling in the militia, which was something they very much did not want to do. They considered the campus almost a separate state, quite superior to the town that surrounded it. But before they were forced to make the fateful decision, a savior appeared.

"A member of the Charlottesville bar, Alexander Rives, an able but eccentric man, without invitation from any one, hurried up from town, and through his influence, the students announced that a meeting of their body would be held at four o'clock that afternoon. In the meanwhile, they promised . . . that they would refrain from all disturbances . . . At four o'clock, about seventy students assembled, and after an address by Rives, who had held no communication with the Faculty or the executive committee, they formally pledged themselves to commit no further breach of the peace."

And so the Calathumpian revolt ended.

Although he obviously held appeal for students, Rives often infuriated everyone else. His family was incensed that he opposed secession, which he had even as a young man. In 1832, when he was only twenty-six, he had written to James Madison, who was then eighty-one, and asked if secession would be legal under the Constitution, as many Virginians—and most of the Rives family—then believed it was. "The opinions of the chief architect of our political systems should not be misconstrued or perverted to sinister purposes," he wrote to Madison. He signed the letter, "A Friend of Union and State Rights." Madison replied that he did not believe a state may "at will" renounce its agreement to remain in the Union. "A rightful secession requires the consent of the others, or an abuse of the compact absolving the seceding party from the obligation imposed by it."

In the decade before war broke out, Rives turned to politics and served in the Virginia state legislature. He left government when Virginia left the Union. Rives remained in Charlottesville during the conflict, never masking his belief that Virginia's secession was illegal. Only his personal reputation likely saved him from violence at the hands of secessionists. After the defeat of the Confederacy, he was appointed to the state's highest court, and then, in 1870, decided to run for Congress as a Republican. He lost but was appointed by President Grant as a federal district court judge. And there he had continued to serve when the Reynolds brothers' motion arrived on his desk.

Rives loathed abuses of power, and in the conviction of Lee Reynolds and the almost conviction of Burwell Reynolds, that is precisely what he saw. Rives declared the trial judge's refusal

to include African Americans in the jury pool a violation of the United States Constitution, in denying them a trial by a jury of their peers. Although he did not put it in those terms, Rives had clearly ignored precedent and used Fourteenth Amendment guarantees to apply the Bill of Rights to the states.

He also decided that simply ordering the trial moved to federal court in Danville, where he sat, would not be enough. So he sent federal marshals to take the brothers into custody and hold them in safety until they could be tried in federal court by a jury that included men of color.

This legal kidnapping of the defendants "created no small stir amongst the bar," newspapers reported. "Its substantial effect is to strip the State courts of their jurisdiction in cases where a negro is tried unless a black jury is empanelled to try him, and looks as if the honorable Judge sought either to force the judges of the State courts to put negroes on their juries or to take the cases from them."

Rives was unperturbed. "In my own court," he said in an

interview, "I have always ordered mixed juries, and have not discovered that any harm resulted from it; on the contrary, the lawyers seem to prefer them."

But a "small stir amongst the bar" was soon replaced by a huge storm of protest. Judge Rives was called a usurper and worse. Rives's "capture" of the Reynolds brothers was called "a flagrant and unconstitutional encroachment upon the exclusive and unquestionable authority of the State." When the Virginia legislature was criticized by a Philadelphia newspaper for announcing that it intended to "look into" the situation, a Virginia newspaper responded that the author was "a man who either regards all the people of the United States as slaves, or else regards the southern people as slaves." White Southerners were quite fond of accusing Northerners of treating them like "slaves," seeming to forget that it was the South, not the North, in which human slavery had been important enough to fight a war over.

Some critics used reason, trying to demonstrate that all-white juries were more fair. "The absurdity of the decision, that a verdict of a white jury against a negro is not good, is scarcely worth while discussing. Judge Rives, in fact, instead of placing the two races on a civil equality, does exactly the reverse, and decides that the whites and negroes have different rights and different privileges—that a white man must have a white jury to try him, a negro a colored jury." Other articles claimed black criminals *begged* to be tried by a white jury.

While reaction in the South was predictable, feelings in the North were often just as extreme. An editor at the *Brooklyn Daily Eagle* wrote that the issue was "whether a colored man, on trial for a criminal offense which is clearly within the exclusive jurisdiction of a State court, has a right to demand a jury composed in whole or in part of men of his own color." He then added, "If such a right exists in Virginia, it also exists in New York." The *Chicago Tribune* described Judge Rives's behavior as "a war on State Courts."

Eventually, the Virginia legislature did take up the matter, and in January 1879, drafted an official twelve-point proclamation denouncing Rives and calling his action "unwarranted by the Constitution" and "destructive of the rights of the people of each State to protect life, liberty, and property in their own way, by their own courts and officers," which "ought at once be remedied by proper judicial action." The governor was "instructed to direct the Attorney-General to institute proceedings in the name of this Commonwealth before the Supreme Court of the United States." Which the attorney general of Virginia proceeded to do.

The key question for the Court, of course, was whether Judge Rives had acted properly in removing the Reynolds brothers to federal jurisdiction. That depended on whether their Fourteenth Amendment rights had been violated, which led directly to Virginia's law governing the selection of potential jurors. In the case of *Strauder*, West Virginia law had restricted jurors to white men; Virginia law did not. Still, for practical purposes, the effect was the same, since Virginia trial judges simply refused to consider African Americans for jury service. Would the Court take into consideration that, whatever Virginia law might have said—or not said—it was clearly being administered in a discriminatory fashion?

The decision, handed down immediately after *Strauder* on March 1, 1880, was unanimous and, as in *Strauder*, was written by Justice Strong.

Strong focused only on language. "It did not assert, nor is it claimed now, that the Constitution or laws of Virginia denied to them any civil right, or stood in the way of their enforcing the equal protection of the laws. The law made no discrimination against them because of their color, nor any discrimination at all . . . It does not exclude colored citizens."

As for the trial judge who "confined his selection to white persons, and refused to select any persons of the colored race, solely because of their color," Strong restated that the Fourteenth Amendment "was intended for [African-Americans'] protection against *State action*, and against *that alone*." And so, "any action [that] was not the state, but a person," such as the trial judge, "was not covered under the Fourteenth Amendment." And so Judge Rives's actions were deemed improper and the Reynolds brothers were ordered returned to state custody.

The impact of the ruling was immense. It told Southern states that they were free to discriminate against American citizens of color—in jury selection, voter registration, or anything else—as long as they did not *announce* it by putting references to race specifically in their laws. It would be a lesson that Southern Democratic governments would learn well.

As with Taylor Strauder, however, the outcome for the Reynolds brothers was unexpected. In June 1880, Burwell Reynolds went on trial in Danville, the very city in which Alexander Rives sat as a federal judge. For reasons never made clear, the state included black men in the jury pool, and four of them were chosen to sit on the jury. That is perhaps why, although Burwell Reynolds was convicted, it was only of manslaughter, a lesser charge than murder. He was sentenced to five years' imprisonment, much lighter than the eighteen years Lee had originally received. Lee Reynolds did even better. The prosecution declined to prosecute him further, and he went free.

CHAPTER 14

BAD SCIENCE AND
BIG MONEY

As THE 1880s PROGRESSED, WHITE supremacists openly and almost gleefully committed voter fraud across the South. In 1900, *on the floor of the United States Senate*, South Carolina senator "Pitchfork Ben" Tillman would brag about the methods used to deny black citizens the vote in those days. "We took the government away. We stuffed ballot boxes. We shot them. We are not ashamed of it."

Still, these same white supremacists felt as much need to justify this behavior as they had to justify slavery. Since even they knew it would not do to enslave equals—or to steal the government from them—they took the position that people of color were, as a race, simply not equal to whites.

But just how they did this evolved. Until the mid-nineteenth century, the favored method was to employ citations from the Bible that were twisted to demonstrate that slavery was actually beneficial to barbaric, childlike Africans. Beginning in about 1840, however, biblical arguments were replaced with "scientific" theories, which "proved" that the black race was demonstrably inferior, unsuited for anything but menial labor, and needing the guiding hand of whites.

The first of these pseudosciences was known as "polygenism," which used a study of human skulls to conclude that blacks and whites had developed separately, from different ancestors. Blacks, then, were not really "human" at all. Polygenism was developed not by a Southerner, but rather by Samuel George Morton from Philadelphia, a physician, geologist, and paleontologist who was hailed as "the most famous American anthropologist of his day." Ethiopians, as he referred to black people, were on the bottom rung of his comparative ladder, "the lowest grade of humanity."

Polygenism became widely accepted and was promoted in the years before the Civil War by Louis Agassiz of Harvard University, thought by many to be the greatest natural scientist in the world. Born and educated in Europe, Agassiz was the first man to suggest that the Earth had undergone an Ice Age. He was equally expert in geology, paleontology, climatology, and ichthyology—the study of fish. With Agassiz as a supporter in the 1850s, whites and especially slave owners finally had the science on which they might deny that black people were human in the same sense as white people. Few Northerners, even those who loathed slavery, would now question the fundamental assertion that African Americans were an inferior race.

Then in 1859, the year before the United States elected Abraham Lincoln president, Charles Darwin, with whom Lincoln shared a birthday—February 12, 1809—published *On the Origin of Species by Means of Natural Selection, or the Preservation of Favoured Races in the Struggle for Life*. From that moment, science changed forever. Around the world, reaction to Darwin's theory

Louis Agassiz.

was so extreme that there are those, even today, who refuse to accept it. In the United States, Agassiz furiously condemned natural selection as "a crude and insolent challenge to the eternal verities, objectionable as science and abominable for its religious blasphemies." But the *New York Times*, in a massive, full-page review of more than four thousand words, gushed, "It is clear that here is one of the most important contributions ever made to philosophic science . . . Ten times the space given to this article would not suffice for any adequate treatment of this vast and complicated subject."

Agassiz's day was done. Neither he nor anyone else could stop Darwin and this new way of looking at how living creatures developed. By the time Agassiz died in 1873, eight of his best students had become Darwinists, including his own son. Polygenism was swept away, just one of many failed theories in the evolution of science.

But polygenism's demise did not mean that acceptance of racial equality would follow. If anything, natural selection, because its foundation was so much more solid and its method so persuasive, would prove a far greater threat to African American equality than polygenism ever had.

Darwin's theory was essentially a five-step process. It began with an individual variation—a "mutation." That variation would be inherited and eventually work its way into the species as "cumulative" variation, a new subspecies. The new and the old would compete for resources in a "struggle for life." That struggle would result in the group more appropriate to its environment winning out over the lesser. These developments were long and slow, taking perhaps thousands of years. And Darwin was making no value judgments. "More appropriate" did not mean "superior." In fact, "superior" and "inferior" were terms that had no place in Darwin's theory. To him, evolution was about adaptability, not quality.

Still, for white supremacists, Darwinism presented an enormous opportunity. If, in civilized society (a definition that could be jiggled to suit), one race or ethnic group did "better" (another definition that could be jiggled to suit), did it not then follow that the more successful group was more suited to civilized society? And the less successful, less suited? Darwin, therefore, had possibly provided scientific justification to society's winners— the rich, the well placed, the powerful . . . and the white.

And since natural selection seemed to say that the inferior species should wither away, then tinkering with the "natural" social order—as Reconstruction wanted to do—could have disastrous consequences. Artificially propping up the less suitable group—which might include the poor, the working class, and the sick, in addition to freed slaves—would corrupt the evolutionary process, and therefore humankind in general. Reconstruction, then, was a threat to the very survival of America.

But before Darwinism could be applied to questions of race or social welfare, it needed someone to extend what Darwin intended to be a theory of biological development to human behavior, to create a "social science" application of what had been meant only as "natural science."

Once more, the man who did so was not a Southern white supremacist, nor this time even an American. He was English and his name was Herbert Spencer.

Spencer, born in 1820, had been a highly gifted student as a child, and as an adult he decided to create a system that could apply the rules of natural science—like biology—to human behavior. He had not been inspired by Darwin—in fact, Spencer began writing of his theory almost a decade before *On the Origin of Species* was published. But with its appearance, Spencer immediately saw Darwin's work as his missing link.

Spencer began with two assumptions. The first was that life-forms, which had begun with simple organisms, such as protozoa and amoebas, had become more and more unique and complex over time, until, finally, the process had created humans, the most unique and complex of all. But even the appearance of *Homo sapiens* had not ended the progression. Humanity itself was evolving from lower to higher forms with "the multiplication of races and the differentiation of these races from each other."

Spencer's second assumption was this process of human evolution toward higher planes of existence would continue only if allowed to do so without interference

Herbert Spencer.

by governments, or by any other effort to artificially support the lower forms. In this he included not only aid for the poor, "but also state-supported education, sanitary supervision . . . regulation of housing conditions, and even state protection of the ignorant against medical quacks." He also left no doubt of what he thought would move humanity on its evolutionary path. "A premium on skill, intelligence, self-control, and the power to adapt through technological innovation . . . had stimulated human advancement and selected the best of each generation for survival." It was Herbert Spencer, not Charles Darwin, who initiated the phrase "survival of the fittest."

Spencer's theories were not specific to race—he would differentiate between poor and rich as readily as between black and white—but, for white supremacists, the message could not have been clearer. Those races or classes that seemed to thrive in modern society could be seen as more suited to modernity than those that did not. Nothing could be more destructive, then, than a concentrated program that aimed to artificially prop up millions of people so inferior—so unfit— that nature had selected them to be slaves.

Spencer's theories came to be known as "Social Darwinism," and they served to unite white supremacists with the immensely wealthy industrial class. Wealth and power became expressions of virtue and progress. The wealthier, the more powerful one became, even at the expense of others—perhaps *especially* at the expense of others—the more he or she was contributing to the advancement of the human race.

When he visited the United States for the first time in 1882, Spencer was hailed as a hero by no less than steel magnate Andrew Carnegie, who "became his intimate friend and showered him with favors." Carnegie would later write a book, *The Gospel of Wealth*, glorifying the values Spencer promoted. Another faithful Spencer admirer was John D. Rockefeller, who once told his Sunday school class, "The growth of a large business is merely a survival of the fittest . . . The American Beauty rose can be produced in the splendor and fragrance which bring cheer to its beholder only by sacrificing the early buds which grow up around it. This is not an evil tendency in business. It is merely the working-out of a law of nature and a law of God." To these men, and many, many others, to oppose evolution, at least Spencer's version, was to oppose progress and the betterment of the human condition.

Spencer would have agreed. He always saw himself as contributing to a more just and even a more charitable existence. He believed that the pursuit of individual wealth led to a society with better conditions for all, with the poor and powerless dragged along in the wake of the ambitious and successful. Some of the less fit would drop away, it was true, but only to allow the more fit to gain a share of resources that, regardless of how prosperous a society might become, would never be sufficient for all.

On first blush, Spencer seems to be well within Darwin's boundaries. If the fittest will survive biologically, why not socially? Does it not follow that the superior will thrive and the inferior fall away? But Darwin's theory is based on *individual* mutations slowly but relentlessly altering a species makeup to allow it to survive in an inhospitable climate. There is no individual mutation in Spencer's world, just an almost instantaneous change of circumstance where one group finds the means to dominate another. Spencer was not describing evolution as much as war; absent total incompetence in command, the superior force will generally win a battle, but that victory hardly guarantees an advancement of the species. In fact, since it is often the brutish and barbarous who triumph in war at the expense of the enlightened and the virtuous, survival of the monied classes might as easily be seen as a step downward rather than a step up.

Social Darwinism was ridiculously flawed and is now mocked as phony science, but at the precise moment that white supremacists were determined to reassert total control of the political process in the South, it gained thousands of fervent disciples in the United States. Social Darwinism had given the Democrats a great gift—the ability to consider themselves virtuous while acting in unconcealed self-interest.

J. Keppler

LOOK
THEY WOULD CLOSE TO THE NEW-COMER

K.

ACKWARD.
THAT CARRIED THEM AND THEIR FATHERS OVER.

J. Ottmann Lith. Co. Puck Building. N.Y.

Cartoon depicting Social Darwinism and immigration. The rich have forgotten their own origins.

For those who would advance the cause of the newly freed slaves, Spencer had created a difficult problem. How could they assert the equality of African Americans without, in the process, denouncing what was rapidly becoming acknowledged as one of the greatest scientific advances in history?

Another problem for those who would promote equal rights was that the prominent Social Darwinists were among the most widely admired men in America. Most ordinary Americans did not see Carnegie, Rockefeller, or the other industrialists as greedy, selfish, or uncaring, but rather as intelligent, innovative, and efficient—what they themselves aspired to become.

And so, even if a man could not be a railroad magnate or a steel baron, he could still gain wealth for himself while helping America and the human race to hurtle forward to previously unimagined glories. Those who toiled in support of capitalists, then—lawyers, for example—could only feel a rush of pride in the knowledge that, while they enriched themselves, they were also enriching society.

A number of those lawyers, including one who was considered by some to be the greatest legal mind in America, found their way to the Supreme Court.

CHAPTER 15

STRANGLING THE CONSTITUTION: THE *CIVIL RIGHTS CASES*

C HALLENGES TO THE CIVIL RIGHTS Act of 1875 reached the Supreme Court in 1880, just after the *Strauder* and *Rives* decisions had been handed down, but Morrison Waite refused to schedule a hearing for another three years. Finally, on March 29, 1883, the justices heard arguments on the five appeals that would be decided together and called the *Civil Rights Cases*.

As the *Chicago Daily Tribune* had predicted, none of the five cases came from the Deep South. One originated in California, where "a colored person [was refused] a seat in the dress circle of Maguire's theatre in San Francisco," and a second in New York City, where "a person, whose color was not stated, [was denied] the full enjoyment of the accommodations of the theatre known as the Grand Opera House." The remaining three cases originated in Missouri, Kansas, and Tennessee.

By the time the cases were heard, the nation's rejection of Reconstruction was near complete. Horatio Seymour, who had narrowly lost the popular vote to Ulysses Grant in 1868, wrote that while he would not "impeach the patriotism" of those who had implemented the Reconstruction programs, "in their eagerness to extend the jurisdiction of the General Government, they went too far, and exposed the country to unforeseen dangers." Seymour was not alone. Even most Republicans had concluded that a good deal of the program had been a mistake. Much of the party had turned against African Americans, and Republican candidates were openly courting white votes in the South. The great historian C. Vann Woodward wrote, "The wing of the Republican party that raised the loudest outcry against Hayes's policy of deserting the Negro promptly abandoned him and threw support to . . . any white independent organization available."

And so, when the Court was finally ready to rule on the constitutionality of the Civil Rights Act of 1875, no one expected it to be much of a contest. And as a matter of law, it was not—the vote was 8–1. But as to a larger question, that of what America should stand for, whether or not honor was as important a national value as power, the *Civil Rights Cases* were quite a contest indeed. The main combatants were two of the justices, Joseph Bradley (representing the eight) and a former Kentucky slaveholder named John Marshall Harlan (the one).

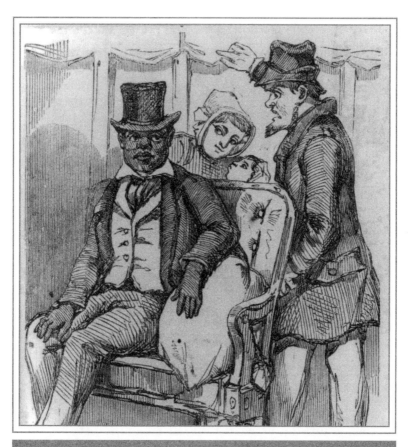

African American ordered to leave a segregated railway car.

Harlan had come to Court to replace now-senator David Davis. At first look, Harlan seemed exactly what those who had accused Hayes of selling out black America would have expected. In addition to being raised in a family of slaveholders, he had opposed the Emancipation Proclamation, spoken out passionately against the three postwar amendments, and, at age twenty-one, had joined the anti-immigrant, antiblack, anti-Catholic, semisecret society called the "Know-Nothings," whose motto was "Put none but Americans on Guard." As Harlan wrote later, "On the evening of my initiation, an oath was administered to me which bound me to vote only for native Americans, and, in effect, only for Protestants." Harlan, at six foot two inches, 240 pounds, with a shock of red hair and a deep, booming delivery, was soon giving speeches all over Kentucky in support of the party's nativist, bigoted agenda.

But Harlan, like Abraham Lincoln, was that rare man who was not afraid of how he might look if he abandoned views he had held since childhood when he realized those views were wrong.

Harlan's conversion began because he opposed secession. He campaigned tirelessly to keep Kentucky loyal—and Kentucky, although a slave state, remained in the Union—and when war did break out, he raised an infantry regiment to fight for the North. He was commissioned into the Union army as a colonel and distinguished himself in battle. Fighting arm in arm with German immigrants and Catholics, Harlan emerged from the war with his Know-Nothing sentiments abandoned.

His views on slavery, however, were unchanged and based on a strong commitment to rights of property holders to not have what they owned taken from them. He opposed the

Thirteenth Amendment on the grounds that it was "a flagrant invasion of the right of self government." He also believed the amendment broke a promise made to the slaveholders of Kentucky who had chosen to remain in the Union, and violated property rights guaranteed by the Constitution.

John Marshall Harlan.

His opinion of the Fourteenth and Fifteenth Amendments was no better, and after the war he joined the Conservative Party. At that point, if forced to choose between the major parties, he would certainly have become a Democrat.

With the presidential nomination of Ulysses Grant, however, Harlan's views changed once more. He had known Grant during the war and respected his toughness and commitment to the United States. Although the Democrats, who dominated Kentucky politics, were urging Harlan to join them and perhaps even to run for office, Harlan instead aligned himself with Grant and the Republicans.

Kentucky Republicans, thrilled to have attracted such a prominent convert, nominated Harlan for governor in 1871.

The only chance he had to win in a heavily Democratic state was to attract a heavy turnout among African Americans—those who could still vote—and so, as in his soldiering days, he found himself getting to know people against whom he had previously been prejudiced. And, again showing his capacity for personal growth, Harlan totally changed his perspective on issues of equal rights.

"I rejoice," announced the man who had opposed the Thirteenth Amendment late in the campaign, "that [slavery] is gone; I rejoice that the Sun of American Liberty does not this day shine upon a single human slave upon this continent; I rejoice that these human beings are now in possession of freedom, and that that freedom is secured to them in the fundamental law of the land, beyond the control of any state." Then he added, noting his attitudes of the past, "Let it be said that I am right rather than consistent."

Harlan lost the election, but he amassed more votes than any other Republican in Kentucky's history. He was nominated again four years later. In this election, the Civil Rights Act of 1875 was a major issue. Of that law, Harlan said, "Under the law of Kentucky, any one of the colored men within the sound of my voice has the same right that any white man possesses to ride in one of your cars from here to the city of Louisville." Harlan lost once more, by an even narrower margin, and, the following year, was instrumental in gaining the presidential nomination for Rutherford B. Hayes. On October 16, 1877, the president nominated him to be associate justice of the Supreme Court. On Thanksgiving Day, 1877, Harlan learned by telegram that he had been confirmed.

In early 1878, John Marshall Harlan took his seat on the high court, set on a collision course with Joseph P. Bradley.

The key question in the *Civil Rights Cases* was once again how much—or how little—the Fourteenth Amendment guaranteed every person in America, no matter the color of their skin, fair and equal treatment under the law. So far the Supreme Court had said the Fourteenth Amendment's protections applied only to actions by a state government, not "private individuals." If a "private individual" violated someone's Fourteenth Amendment rights, the federal government could do nothing.

But what about people who worked for the state—a voting registrar, for example, or a state judge? If one of them, in his or her official capacity, violated a person's Fourteenth Amendment rights, could *that* be corrected by federal action? In other words, were the officials who refused to enforce the Civil Rights Act, and, by extension, who denied qualified African Americans the right to vote, "states" or "private individuals" in the eyes of the law?

Logic would seem to suggest the people acting for the state *were* the state. After all, without the people, a state becomes just land, water, and buildings, and no one suggested that the Fourteenth Amendment be limited to those. But although logic said one thing, the justices had more than once demonstrated they might decide the law said another.

There was another factor. Sometimes two passages in the Constitution seem to be in conflict with each other. When that happens, the Supreme Court will usually have to decide which one takes precedence over the other. In this case, two amendments, the Fourteenth and the Tenth, seemed to be in opposition. The Fourteenth Amendment, of course, seemed to give the federal government the power to decide if a state law denied "equal protection" or "due process" to its citizens. The Tenth Amendment, however, had been added to the Constitution to limit the power of the federal government to tell states what to do. It reads, "The powers not delegated to the United States by the Constitution, nor prohibited by it to the States, are reserved to the States respectively, or to the people." Nowhere in the Constitution is a passage that specifically gives the federal government the right to overturn a state law because it didn't provide "equal protection" or "due process."

So which of these amendments outweighed the other?

Ordinarily, a law that was passed later—in this case, the Fourteenth Amendment—canceled out an earlier law—in this case, the Tenth. And that was exactly what Solicitor General Samuel F. Phillips argued. He said that the Fourteenth Amendment defined new areas—judging equal protection and due process—that were "delegated to the United States." Congress therefore had the power to pass laws to ensure equal treatment of all citizens, since this power was no longer reserved to the states. (This is the view of the Fourteenth Amendment that in large part we hold today.)

But the Waite Court was not certain to agree. The justices seemed to believe that only states could pass laws concerning equal rights. For example, the Court had ruled that the Fourteenth Amendment did not apply the Bill of Rights to the states. That meant states alone could decide whether First Amendment rights such as freedom of speech, freedom of religion, freedom of the press, or the right of the people to peaceably assemble would apply within their borders. (Today, all of these rights are mandatory in every state in America.)

And so, attorneys for the defendants in the *Civil Rights Cases*, those who had denied African Americans access to public facilities, argued that Congress had no right to enact equal rights legislation. Only states could do that—if they chose to. They accused Solicitor General Phillips of trying to use the Fourteenth Amendment to achieve social goals that neither Congress, when it passed the amendment, nor the

Constitution had ever intended. They neglected to mention that the men who drafted the Fourteenth Amendment had made it plain that they meant to do precisely that.

That left the Court to decide down which path the nation would travel. With the law so imprecise, the justices could find support in any interpretation of the Constitution they chose. And, through Justice Bradley, they chose to support white supremacy.

Bradley began by restating that the Fourteenth Amendment was only binding on the states. He wrote that the Fourteenth Amendment did "not invest Congress with power to legislate upon subjects which are within the domain of State legislation;" (in other words, "ordinary people") "but to provide modes of relief against State legislation, or State action." In case that wasn't clear enough, he added, "Individual invasion of individual rights is not the subject matter of the amendment." Since the defendants in each of the five cases were all private business owners, only the states could regulate their behavior. That made the Civil Rights Act of 1875 an unconstitutional incursion on the rights of states, not justified by the Fourteenth Amendment. The law was therefore unconstitutional and must be struck down.

Although there was no need to do so, Bradley had made a point of defining state employees as "ordinary people" as well.

According to his definition, "subjects which are within the domain of State legislation" would include, say, voting registrars and state judges. As a result, unless a state law made a point of discriminating against African Americans—actually declared that it would do so—the Fourteenth Amendment was just a string of useless sentences.

The decision and the legal reasoning surprised no one. The Court had been creating precedent for this decision for years. But then Bradley did something unexpected. Seemingly unable to restrain himself, he added commentary on the entire effort to obtain equal rights for black Americans.

Solicitor General Phillips had tried to make the point that discriminating against someone because of skin color was the sort of thing that had been done to slaves. He called such behavior "badges of servitude," which were prohibited by the Thirteenth Amendment. It was not a very strong argument— not all discrimination is slavery—and Bradley wasn't buying it. "It would be running the slavery argument into the ground," he wrote, "to make it apply to every act of discrimination which a person may see fit to make as to the guests he will entertain, or as to the people he will take into his coach or cab or car, or admit to his concert or theatre, or deal with in other matters of intercourse or business."

If he had stopped there, Bradley's opinion might have been seen as simply adherence to a debatable legal philosophy, but he did not stop there. In stunningly pompous language, he revealed the blind racism that was at the core of his reasoning. "When a man has emerged from slavery, and, by the aid of beneficent legislation, has shaken off the inseparable concomitants of that state, there must be some stage in the progress of his eleva-

Joseph P. Bradley.

tion when he takes the rank of a mere citizen and *ceases to be the special favorite of the laws*, and when his rights as a citizen or a man are to be protected in the ordinary modes by which other men's rights are protected."

That a justice of the United States Supreme Court could make such a statement in the face of literally thousands of incidents of beatings, murder, rape, and intimidation of African Americans by whites—despite the reign of terror waged by the Ku Klux Klan and other violent Redeemer groups; despite the most obvious ploys to deny the vote instituted by whites against blacks; despite vagrancy laws, rigged juries, and rampant violation of contract rights—is simply astounding.

This, however, seemed the Court's point all along. The justices who concurred with Bradley had all but announced that they, as well as the white population they represented, wanted to be out of the business of protecting a class of Americans whom they held to be of no value. Stop complaining to us, Bradley seemed to be saying.

But then there was the one. At the same inkstand that Chief Justice Roger B. Taney had written the infamous *Dred Scott* opinion, John Marshall Harlan, the former slave owner from Kentucky, wrote what was to become one of the most praised opinions in the history of the Supreme Court.

"I cannot resist the conclusion that the substance and spirit of the recent amendments of the Constitution have been sacrificed by a subtle and ingenious verbal criticism," Harlan began. Then he quoted Edmund Plowden, a famed English legal theorist who in 1574 wrote words that are as important today as they were 450 years ago. "It is not the words of the law, but the internal sense of it that makes the law; *the letter of the law is the body; the sense and reason of the law is the soul.*"

Harlan chided his colleagues for ignoring what those who enacted the amendments had intended to achieve. "Constitutional provisions, adopted in the interest of liberty and for the purpose of securing, through national legislation, if need be, rights inhering in a state of freedom and belonging to

American citizenship have been so construed as to defeat the ends the people desired to accomplish, which they attempted to accomplish, and which they supposed they had accomplished by changes in their fundamental law . . . The court has departed from the familiar rule requiring . . . that full effect be given to the intent with which they were adopted."

But he saved his harshest words for Bradley's argument that African Americans were "special favorites of the laws." "What the nation, through congress, has sought to accomplish in reference to that race is, *what had already been done in every state in the Union for the white race*, to secure and protect rights belonging to them as freemen and citizens; nothing more. The one underlying purpose of congressional legislation has been to enable the black race to take the rank of mere citizens. The difficulty has been to compel a recognition of their legal right to take that rank, and to secure the enjoyment of privileges belonging, under the law, to them as a component part of the people for whose welfare and happiness government is ordained."

Harlan closed with this famous passage: "Today it is the colored race which is denied by corporations and individuals . . . rights fundamental in their freedom and citizenship. At some future time, it may be that some other race will fall under the ban of race discrimination. *If the constitutional amendments be enforced according to the intent with which . . . they were adopted,*

there cannot be, in this republic, any class of human beings in prac-
tical subjection to another class . . . The supreme law of the land
has decreed that no authority shall be exercised in this country upon the basis of discrimination . . . against freemen and
citizens because of their race, color, or previous condition of
servitude."

History may have praised Justice Harlan, but at the time,
most of white America did not. Harlan's ideals were as unwel-
come in the North as in the South. The *New York Times*,
pleased to find accurate its prediction that the Court would
overturn the law, wrote in an editorial that "the whole matter is now remanded to State authority in which it rightfully
belongs." The author added that "it is doubtful if social privileges can be successfully dealt with by legislation of any kind."
But, the *New York Times* pointed out, all too correctly, "The
decision is unlikely to have any considerable practical impact,
for the reason that the act of 1875 has never been enforced. The
general practice of railroads, hotels and theatres has remained
unchanged and has depended mainly on the prevailing sentiment of the communities in which they are located."

The *Brooklyn Daily Eagle* agreed. "There was a time when
this decision would have created some excitement, but that
time passed years ago . . . The Negro gained nothing by the
passage of the Civil Rights act, and he will lose nothing by
having it declared a dead letter. The decision simply gives

him notification . . . that his advancement from a position of mere dependency on his white neighbor was to be brought about, not by fulminations of politicians but by self-respect, patience, hard work and general good behavior on his own part." The editor also observed, "The decision is interesting as another proof that the Supreme Court continues to be . . . true to the spirit and structure of our Government . . . There, if nowhere else . . . loyalty to the fundamental law of the land has found a home."

Southern newspapers were gleeful. The *Atlanta Journal-Constitution* proclaimed in a headline, "A Radical Relic Rubbed Out. Special Rights for None but Equal Rights for All. A Triumph of Law and Sense Which Strengthens the Decree That the Republicans Must Go."

Not every white newspaper praised the decision. The *Hartford Courant* wrote sadly, "We regret that the judicial authority of the land has felt a duty . . . to wipe out of existence a law that for nearly ten years has worked no harm to anybody, and has been a testimony on the part of the American people of their sincerity in demanding equal rights for all men." Of course, most of white America had done no such thing.

Black newspapers were unanimous in their outrage at the decision. The *Boston Hub* charged that the Court had deliberately cast the power of the judiciary against equal rights. The *Louisville Bulletin* exclaimed, "Our government is a farce, and a snare, and the sooner it is overthrown and an empire established upon its ruins the better." The *New York Globe* denounced Bradley as reaffirming the "infamous decision of infamous Chief Justice Taney [in *Dred Scott*] that 'a black man has no rights that a white is bound to respect.'"

One of the most interesting reactions came from William Strong, a former justice who had retired to reenter private practice. He wrote to Justice Harlan, "At first I was inclined to agree with the Court but since reading your opinion, I am in great doubt. It may be that you are right. The opinion of the Court, as you said, is too narrow—sticks to the letter, while you aim to bring out the Spirit of the Constitution."

CHAPTER 16

THE WINDOW CRACKS OPEN: THE CURIOUS INCIDENT OF THE CHINESE LAUNDRY AND EQUAL PROTECTION

ALTHOUGH THE COURT HAD NOT addressed specifically whether a man or woman working for the state was an "ordinary person" with respect to the Fourteenth Amendment, it seemed clear from the *Civil Rights Cases* that the justices believed they were, that no matter what action they took to deny equal rights to American citizens, they could only be punished—or even stopped—if the state that employed them chose to do so. Even worse, if the state *approved* of their behavior, the federal government still could do nothing to protect those who had been wronged. Three years later, however, it appeared that perhaps the justices might be prepared to see things a bit differently. It came about from another of the oddest cases in Supreme Court history, one that began with precious metal and ended with soapsuds.

On January 24, 1848, a carpenter named James Marshall was supervising the construction of a sawmill for John Sutter near the American Fork River in north central California. He noticed some metal flakes near a stream. The flakes were gold.

Most of the crew quit immediately and set themselves to prospecting. Sutter tried to kick them off his land without making a fuss—if word got out, he would be overrun. His former workmen did their best not to publicize their activities, to avoid being overrun themselves. But gold is a secret not easily kept and word began to leak out. By the following year, a full-blown Gold Rush had begun.

Upwards of eighty thousand would-be millionaires descended on California. San Francisco's population exploded, growing from about eight hundred people in 1848 to twenty-five thousand just two years later. Most came overland or by steamship from the east, but others came from across the Pacific, almost all of them from China. Most Chinese arrived intending to stay only long enough at "Gold Mountain" to allow them to return home rich. At first, the hardworking Chinese were accepted by the other miners. But as gold became scarcer and Chinese prospectors became more plentiful—there would be twenty-four thousand within three years—resentment developed.

In 1850, California began taxing "foreign" miners. Most immigrant whites avoided paying by simply saying they were

American, but Chinese miners did not have the same option. Of those Chinese miners who did pay the tax, many became victims of violence by white men.

As a result, most Chinese miners gave up the hunt for gold and entered other professions. Some hired themselves out as workers in mining camps, some became farm laborers, while still others settled in cities—mostly in booming San Francisco—and sought to open their own businesses. One obvious opportunity was in laundering. Most of the men who arrived in California to hunt for gold came alone. Mining was dirty, dusty work, but washing grimy, mud-caked clothes was considered a "woman's

PACIFIC CHIVALRY.
Encouragement to Chinese Immigration.

Anti-Chinese cartoon.

job." Within a few years, the Chinese came to dominate the laundry business in San Francisco.

By the 1870s, Chinese immigration had continued to increase and the white population grew more and more determined to halt what they saw as pollution by an inferior race. Chinese laborers were key targets, since they were seen as lowering wages for white workers. Another focus was Chinese women, who were assumed to be prostitutes. In 1875, Horace Page, a California Republican, sponsored a bill to "end the danger of cheap Chinese labor and immoral Chinese women." The Page Act was the first law in American history that restricted the entry of specific "undesirable" elements.

At the same time, California enacted a series of laws aimed at denying Chinese immigrants, almost none of whom were citizens, either employment or housing. For example, an 1870 San Francisco law called "The Sanitary Ordinance" said that all housing must have five hundred cubic feet of air for each occupant. The law was enforced only in Chinatown, where immigrants, most of whom were working for impossibly low wages, lived in horribly cramped conditions. Many Chinese immigrants who could not pay the steep fines were sent to equally overcrowded local jails.

Although few Chinese immigrants could speak English, they acquired a sophisticated understanding of the American legal system. Each time California passed a discriminatory

Chinese laundry, 1881.

law, Chinese businessmen hired white lawyers to bring suit in either state or federal court. And they generally won. A key case, in 1879, involved a law that ordered all male prisoners to have their hair cut to one inch of their scalps. This was an extraordinary humiliation of Chinese prisoners, since the "queue," the long braid worn down their backs, was required in their society as a sign of respect to the Qing emperor. Failure to wear the queue meant death, so any man with his hair shorn could not return to China. (That preventing an immigrant from returning home was an odd way to shrink the Chinese population did not seem to have occurred to the city fathers.) When a laborer named Ah Kow was jailed under the Sanitary Ordinance, and then had his hair shorn, his lawyers contested both his imprisonment and what had become known as the "Pigtail Law."

The law was upheld in state court, so Ah Kow's lawyer appealed to federal court, where Supreme Court Justice Stephen Field was sitting on circuit. (In those days, each Supreme Court justice would also preside over circuit court twice a year.) Field was the most pro-business of all the members of the Court and had dissented in the *Slaughter-House Cases*, siding with the butchers' right to work where, when, and however they pleased.

In *Ah Kow v. Nunan*, Field, who was from California and whose personal views in no way favored the Chinese, voided Ah Kow's conviction and declared the California law unconstitutional. Field's reasoning was what made the decision so important. Calling the Sanitary Ordinance "spiteful and hateful," he wrote, "The equality of protection thus assured to every one whilst within the United States, from whatever country he may have come, or of whatever race or color he may be, implies . . . that the courts of the country shall be open to him on the same terms as to all others."

Never before had the Fourteenth Amendment guarantee of "equal protection of the law" been used to void a state or federal statute. Just as important was Field's assertion that Fourteenth Amendment protections were not reserved for the native-born, since the text read "any person" and not "any citizen."

But Field's opinion was pushing against a very strong tide. Three years later, in 1882, Congress passed and President Chester Arthur signed the Chinese Exclusion Act, which denied entry into the United States to Chinese laborers. It was the first immigration law passed in the United States that restricted immigration of a specific national or ethnic group. The Chinese Exclusion Act was broadly applied and halted virtually all Chinese immigration for almost a century.

The *Ah Kow* decision did not put an end to anti-Chinese legislation in California. In 1880, San Francisco passed a law that required all laundries operating within the city limits and not constructed of brick or stone to obtain a special operating license. This, the city claimed, was because of the extreme fire hazard created by laundries housed in wooden buildings. At the time, there were 320 laundries in San Francisco, all but ten wood framed. Ninety percent of all the city's buildings were, in fact, of wood construction.

After the law took effect, 280 license applications were submitted. Eighty were granted—all to white owners; 200 were denied—all but one for Chinese owners. Not one Chinese laundry owner was granted a license.

One of those denied was the proprietor of the Yick Wo laundry. The proprietor's name is uncertain—it may have been Lee Yick—but he had come to the United States in 1861 and had been operating his business for twenty-two years. Like many Chinese immigrants, he had never become a United States citizen. Although the Yick Wo laundry had passed inspections by both the fire wardens and the health department, the proprietor was ordered to close his business down. When he refused, Sheriff Peter Hopkins arrested him. Not caring enough to find out the actual identity of the man he had brought to the station, Hopkins simply booked the man as Yick Wo.

When "Yick Wo" refused to pay the mandated ten-dollar fine, he was sent to jail for ten days. Hopkins arrested 150 other Chinese laundry owners who refused to close their shops, and almost all of them were sent to jail as well.

But the Chinese Laundryman's Guild, the Tung Hing Tong, had become a powerful force in the city and, to contest the arrests, they hired Hall McAllister, the best and highest-paid lawyer in San Francisco.

McAllister had come to San Francisco from Georgia in the 1870s to sell dry goods to miners but soon saw that there was more money in law. His first case had been representing a group of sailors whose captain had refused to pay them for the voyage from New York—he said they had signed on for a round trip and they would get paid when the ship returned. The sailors insisted the captain had promised to pay them half in San Francisco and owed them $1,000.

In court, the captain presented a contract signed by each member of the crew, and sure enough, it appeared that the seamen had agreed to forgo payment until the ship docked in New York. But McAllister noticed something odd and when he held the pages up to the light, the judge could see that some of the original writing had been carefully erased and different text inserted in its place.

McAllister won the case. The sailors paid him half, $500. He was twenty-three years old, and off and running.

In a boomtown like San Francisco, there were always swindles, frauds, misappropriations of funds, and violations of contract awaiting a good lawyer. Word got around and McAllister was soon buried in an avalanche of legal work. In his first full year as an attorney, he earned $150,000—almost $3 million today.

McAllister's father followed his son to San Francisco, and three years later, using his son's connections, was nominated by President Franklin Pierce as a federal circuit court judge. After he was confirmed, he regularly heard cases in which his son was one of the lawyers. The elder McAllister appointed another son, Cutler, as clerk of the court.

Even with all that clout, Hall McAllister lost the first round in the laundry case—the California supreme court sided with the city. McAllister appealed—although not to his father—and in early January 1886, *Yick Wo v. Hopkins* reached the United States Supreme Court.

Yick Wo was not the first case that the Court had heard regarding discrimination against Chinese laundrymen in California. In January 1885, the Court had ruled on an equal protection case challenging a San Francisco law prohibiting laundries from operating between ten o'clock at night and six in the morning. Night washing, drying, and especially ironing, was a fire hazard, according to the Board of Supervisors, and the law was to protect "public health and public safety." But Chinese launderers were the only ones who worked through the night, so they were the only ones arrested and prosecuted. They claimed that the law targeted them alone, as in *Ah Kow*, but the Court, in a unanimous opinion authored by Field himself, disagreed.

Field wrote that the Fourteenth Amendment does not interfere with a state's right "to prescribe regulations to promote the health, safety, peace, morals, education, good order, and general welfare of its people." That "a special burden" happened to be placed on "a certain class" did not mean that it denied the equal protection of the law, "as special burdens are often necessary for the general welfare." A state or city had the right to decide how businesses or trades should be regulated and "every presumption is to be indulged in favor of the validity of such a statute." In other words, a state or city could do pretty much as it pleased as long as a law was written to apply to everyone equally.

Two months later, the Court once again unanimously ruled, again through Justice Field, that the night work prohibition was a legitimate exercise of the city's power to regulate, and that the Court was in no position to rule on the *motives* of those who enacted the law, even though some had made public statements that it was directed against the Chinese. But Field added something in this decision that had not been present in the first. "The principal objection of the petitioner to the ordinance in question is founded upon the supposed *hostile motives* of the supervisors in passing it," Field wrote, but "even if the motives of the supervisors were as alleged, the ordinance would not be thereby changed from a legitimate police regulation *unless in its enforcement it is made to operate only against the class mentioned.*"

It was in that final sentence that Hall McAllister saw his opening. A law written to apply to all but enforced only against one "class" might violate the equal protection clause. And in the *Yick Wo* case, selective enforcement could not have been more obvious. "It's not rocket science," Justice

Anthony Kennedy observed later, "to figure out that something was drastically wrong." So McAllister based his appeal on the claim that Yick Wo and the other Chinese launderers had been denied their Fourteenth Amendment rights in "a system of oppression to one kind of men and favoritism to all others."

The Court rendered its verdict on May 10, 1886. The decision was once again unanimous, Justice Stanley Matthews writing the opinion. Matthews began by denying precedent of night work cases, which, he said, involved an ordinance that applied to all launderers equally—even though only the Chinese launderers worked through the night. This case was different. The law in question gave *arbitrary* power to the supervisors to decide who could remain in business and who could not. (The behavior of voting registrars had and would continue to be an important factor in voting rights cases.) Although Yick Wo and his co-petitioners "complied with every requisite deemed by the law or by the public officers charged with its administration necessary for the protection of neighboring property from fire or as a precaution against injury to the public health," they were ordered to close their businesses. "And while this consent of the supervisors is withheld from them and from two hundred others who have also petitioned, all of whom happen to be Chinese subjects, eighty others, not Chinese subjects, are permitted to carry on the same business under similar conditions."

As such, Matthews concluded, the California law was applied "with an evil eye and an unequal hand." In an additional wrinkle that would have enormous impact later, that Yick Wo and his co-petitioners were not citizens did not matter. "The Fourteenth Amendment to the Constitution is not confined to the protection of citizens. It says: 'Nor shall any state deprive any *person* of life, liberty, or property, without due process of law; nor deny to any *person* within its jurisdiction the equal protection of the laws.'" The judgments of the lower courts were therefore reversed and Yick Wo and the other launderers were set free.

From there, Yick Wo and his fellows disappeared into history. For Hall McAllister, however, the victory in Washington capped a brilliant career and cemented his place as one of San Francisco's most prominent citizens. McAllister died two years later, on December 1, 1888. On April 15, 1905, a thousand people stood in the rain to see a statue of him unveiled near San Francisco City Hall and hear him praised as the "foremost advocate" of the city's bar. The statue still stands.

Yick Wo v. Hopkins has long been considered one of the nation's most important civil rights rulings, cited more than 150 times in subsequent Supreme Court opinions in cases ranging from apportionment to jury selection to loitering.

Statue of Hall McAllister in San Francisco.

For those seeking to advocate for equal rights for African Americans, especially those fighting a white supremacist power structure in a Redeemed South, *Yick Wo* seemed to provide a weapon of vast potential, if only the justices were willing to use the same standards in protecting their rights as the Court had in protecting Chinese laundrymen.

CHAPTER 17

CORRUPT REDEMPTION: THE 1890 MISSISSIPPI CONSTITUTION

BY 1890, THROUGH TERROR AND voter fraud, white supremacists had successfully taken back control of every state in the old Confederacy. Although African Americans were legally entitled to vote and many continued to try, they could not do so in sufficient numbers to affect most outcomes. Still, many white Democrats were uneasy at the widespread and even casual reliance on illegal methods. A Mississippi judge named J. J. Chrisman observed, "It is no secret that there has not been a full vote and a fair count in Mississippi since 1875. In plain words, we have been stuffing the ballot boxes, committing perjury, and here and there in the state carrying the elections by fraud and violence until the whole machinery for elections was about to rot down."

It was not that white people minded using terror and fraud. But many realized that these might prove unreliable if the mood of the nation changed and Americans—even

Democrats—began to demand honest elections. So, taking a lesson from the Radical Republicans, who had used—or at least attempted to use—the United States Constitution to guarantee equal rights, white supremacists in the South decided to use state constitutions to guarantee unequal rights. State constitutions were subject to review by the United States Supreme Court, of course, but the Court had been very cooperative in endorsing the return to white rule in the South. There was *Yick Wo*, but it remained to be seen whether the justices would use the laundry case as precedent when it was African American voters and not businesspeople they would be protecting.

And so, in February 1890, with the encouragement of United States senator James Z. George, the Mississippi legislature passed a resolution calling for a constitutional convention to meet in Jackson in August 1890, with elections for delegates held one month before. To ensure the new constitution's adoption, the state legislature changed a law that required the document be submitted to the voters and instead allowed a vote among the very delegates who had drawn it up to be sufficient.

Although a number of states in the old Confederacy had drafted new constitutions after the army had withdrawn and Democrats had taken over, Mississippi would be the first state to hold a constitutional convention for the express purpose of denying the vote to African Americans. Democrats made little secret of their intent. James K. Vardaman, later to be elected both governor and United States senator, observed, "There is no use to equivocate or lie about the matter. Mississippi's constitutional convention of 1890 was held for no other purpose than to eliminate the nigger from politics . . . let the world know it just as it is."

James K. Vardaman.

But just how to accomplish this was a bit trickier than it might have seemed. While almost no white people wanted African Americans to actually vote in Mississippi, they were split on whether or not men of color should be *registered* to vote. That was because in parts of the state with large black populations, white people had been using black registration to stuff ballot boxes and elevate the vote count for Democrats. On the state level, this meant that "black belt" counties, as they were called, would have more representation in the state legislature than they would if black men were taken off the voting rolls.

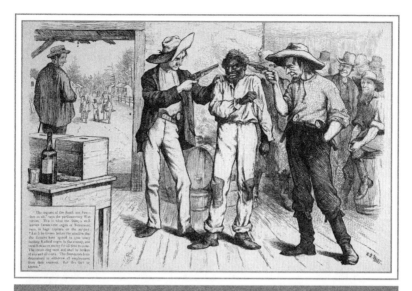

"Of course he wants to vote the Democratic ticket." Voter intimidation in the South.

Then there was the question of poor and illiterate white voters. Since the new constitution had to *appear* not to discriminate, any provision that would be used to deny black men the right to register might also eliminate a good many white voters. Many of Mississippi's wealthier whites would not have minded seeing the influence of poor farmers decrease, but those in government who came from poor districts wanted to keep them on the rolls.

And so the path Senator George and his fellow delegates had to navigate had some twists and turns. But George was the perfect man to lead them through the thicket. Like John A. Campbell, James Z. George had a first-rate legal mind

that he had decided to
use in the pursuit of white
supremacy. And his cre-
dentials with Mississippi
Democrats were impec-
cable. He had served in
the Mexican War under
Colonel Jefferson Davis,
and then as a colonel himself in the Civil War, where
he was captured and spent

Senator James Z. George.

two years in a Yankee prison. After the war, he practiced law,
gaining enough of a reputation that in 1879 he was chosen to
be chief justice of the Mississippi supreme court. Two years
later, he was appointed to the United States Senate, replacing
Republican Blanche K. Bruce, the only African American up
to that time to serve out a full six-year term. When the call for
a convention came, George was perhaps the most respected
man in Mississippi, at least among its white residents.

George had always been a champion of the small farmer—
he was known as the "Great Commoner"—and so as the
election of delegates neared, most Mississippi Democrats
agreed to find a way to deny the vote to African Americans
while not disqualifying illiterate whites. These same issues
existed throughout the South, so other Confederate states

watched what was unfolding in Mississippi with great interest. A prominent newspaper proclaimed, "The eye of the country is on Mississippi."

Mississippi Republicans were in a difficult spot. There was no question that the vast majority of delegates would be Democrats—most ran unopposed—but Republicans were hoping for *some* representation, if for no other reason than to challenge the constitution in court later.

A movement began, particularly among African Americans, to try to elect as many delegates to the convention as possible. The difficulty, of course, was that in a state where voting fraud was as common as magnolias, Democrats had no difficulty ensuring a rigged election. Terror was also freely employed. Marsh Cook, a white Republican campaigning to be a delegate, was ambushed and murdered on a country road in Jasper County. No one was arrested. In the end, of the 137 delegates chosen to attend the convention, only two were Republicans. One of them, Isaiah Montgomery, was a wealthy black landowner who had agreed to support tightened voting eligibility.

When the convention met, the question of just how to remove African Americans from the rolls was raised again. Even though the United States Supreme Court had been a friend to white supremacists, there were more than a few delegates who feared attacking black voting head-on. They decided that a possible alternative to decreasing the black

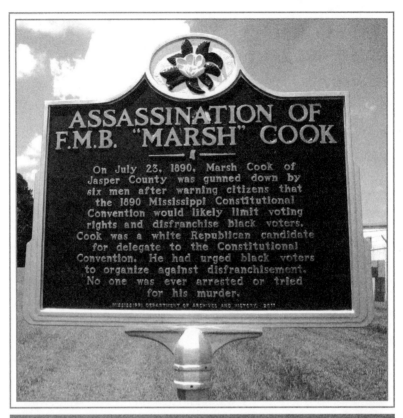

vote was to increase the white vote. And so an extraordinary proposal made the rounds—to open the vote to women. Only white women, of course, for which qualifications could easily be drafted. Mississippi might then be considered the most progressive state in the nation, rather than the most racist. Women's suffrage gained some serious consideration before being rejected for more traditional means.

With James George writing much of the draft, the new constitution's voting qualifications included a two-year residency requirement, an annual poll tax, and a requirement that an applicant must read and interpret a section of the state constitution chosen by a local official. Just what that section would be, or if the same section had to be chosen for black and white voters, was not specified. Since a complete, statewide reregistration of voters was also required, the "understanding and interpretation" clause could be used not only to prevent new registration by African Americans, but also to disqualify those already on the rolls. While white voters were given extremely simple clauses to read (and were often helped along by agreeable poll workers), African Americans were given dense, largely incomprehensible passages, which had been written for that very purpose. (During his campaign for reelection in 1946, Mississippi senator Theodore Bilbo observed, "The poll tax won't keep 'em [blacks] from voting. What keeps 'em from voting is section 244 of the constitution of 1890 that Senator George wrote. It says that a man, to register, must be able to read and explain the constitution when read to him . . . And then Senator George wrote a constitution that damn few white men and no niggers at all can explain.")

Within a few years, George, Vardaman, and the rest of the Democrats had scored an almost total victory. African Americans had largely disappeared from the lists of registered

Mocking the literacy test.

voters. (Since they were still counted in the census, Mississippi kept the same number of congressmen as when black men had the vote, only now they were all Democrats.) And, of course, when African Americans were no longer on the voting lists, they would be stricken from jury rolls as well.

Success breeds imitation, and so, one by one, every Southern state either redrafted or amended its constitution to keep men of color out of the voting booth.

In 1898, for example, Louisiana convened a constitutional convention to, in the words of one state politician, "establish the supremacy of the white race." Like the Mississippi plan, there was no mention of race, but the intent could not have been more clear. There were three different ways in which an adult could register to vote. The first was the ability to read and write and to fill out an application form without assistance. The Louisiana courts ruled that a perfectly filled-out application was needed to satisfy this requirement. Since most former slaves were either illiterate or semiliterate, they were unable to qualify. (The "without assistance" part was largely ignored. As in Mississippi, voting officials often helped illiterate whites.) Alternately, an applicant might demonstrate ownership of property assessed at least at $300, and produce a record of paying property taxes. Once again, very few black Louisianans could qualify, nor could many whites. To make certain that their new constitution denied suffrage only to African Americans, there was the "grandfather clause," which obviously applied only to white voters, since recently freed slaves were extremely unlikely to have had parents or grandparents eligible to vote before the date indicated. As always, the clause made no mention of race.

No male person who was on January 1st, 1867, or at any date prior thereto, entitled to vote under the Constitution or statutes of any State of the United States, wherein he then resided, and no son or grandson of any such person not less than twenty-one years of age at the date of the adoption of this Constitution . . . shall be denied the right to register and vote in this State by reason of his failure to possess the educa-tional or property qualifications prescribed by this Constitution.

Also as in Mississippi, the 1898 Louisiana constitution was not submitted to the voters for ratification but simply adopted by the delegates to the convention that drew it up.

Once again, the results were all that Democrats could have hoped for. Official Louisiana records state that on "January 1, 1897, Number of Negro voters 130,344, Number of White voters 164,088. On March 17, 1900 Negro 5,320 White 125,437." The numbers were broken down further as to the qualifications under which these voters registered in 1900. "Under the 'educational' qualification: White 86,157; Negro 4,327. Under the 'property' qualification: White 10,793; Negro 916. Under the 'grandfather' clause: White, 29,189; Negro, 0."

South Carolina adopted a constitution in 1895 that required a literacy test and a poll tax, and disqualified from voting anyone convicted of crimes of which many African Americans were charged but few whites. That constitution also, for the first time, made school segregation a state law. "Separate schools shall be provided for children of white and colored races, and no child of either race shall ever be permitted to attend a school provided for children of the other race." It also prohibited "marriage of a white person with a Negro or mulatto or a person who shall have one-eighth or more of Negro blood." (Laws preventing marriage between the races remained on the books until 1967, when in *Loving v. Virginia*, a unanimous decision by the Supreme Court written by Chief Justice Earl Warren, who thirteen years before had written the opinion in *Brown v. Board of Education*, ruled that prohibiting interracial marriage was a violation of the due process and equal protection clauses of the Fourteenth Amendment.)

North Carolina chose the amendment route. In January 1899, after those who had been elected in the corrupt election of 1898 had assumed their seats in the state assembly, and the Wilmington invaders had been allowed to stay in

Josephus Daniels riding with President Franklin D. Roosevelt in 1940.
His racist past did not seem to bother many Northerners.

their stolen jobs, Democrats moved to end African American participation in government. As with other white supremacists across the South, Josephus Daniels, who was later to serve eight years as secretary of the navy, made no attempt to hide what Democrats had in mind. "There is no half-way ground in a revolution such as we have passed through. No election law can permanently preserve White Supremacy . . . As long as 120,000 negroes stand united, with their names on the registration books, the sword of bad government hangs ready to fall upon our heads." He added that white supremacy could only be achieved by "a constitutional amendment that will disfranchise the mass of black voters." Unlike in other Southern states, however, North Carolina Democrats were also willing, even eager, to take the vote from the white farmers who had supported the Fusionists.

In 1900, after the amendment had passed, but before it could fully take effect, Democrat Charles Aycock, who had played an important role in Wilmington, won the governor's race by 60,000 votes, with more than 300,000 voters casting ballots. Four years later, in the next election for governor, another Democrat, Robert Glenn, was elected by an almost 2–1 margin, but only 200,000 voters went to the polls—only 50 percent of those who should have been eligible. Almost none of them were black.

With the federal government providing no assistance, and state governments now their enemy, those who wished to fight for racial justice had no choice but to try once more to sway the Supreme Court. Two remarkable African Americans would lead the way. One's fame has survived for more than a century; the other has been lost to history.

CHAPTER 18

THE CRUSADER:
WILLIAMS V. MISSISSIPPI

I N DECEMBER 1895, TWO DAYS after Christmas, the body
of Eliza Brown was discovered under a pile of cloth-
ing in the shack in which she lived in Washington County,
Mississippi. She had been strangled, and her live-in lover,
Henry Williams, had disappeared. Williams, like Taylor
Strauder, was a jealous man and had told friends that Eliza
had been unfaithful. Although there were no witnesses or
any physical evidence linking Williams to the crime, he was
immediately sought as the prime suspect. A few days later, he
was found hiding in an attic and arrested.

Williams said that when he had arrived home on Christmas
day, he had seen another man leaving, although he could not
identify the man nor did any other evidence of the visitor turn
up. But he denied killing Eliza Brown.

If Henry Williams had been white, it might have been
possible to plant some doubt in jurors' minds, but a domestic
killing by a black man did not promise to result in anything

but a brief trial followed by a verdict of guilty by an all-white jury. And so it was. On June 16, 1896, Williams was convicted of murder and sentenced to hang.

Under most circumstances, the execution would have proceeded without fuss or fanfare. But Henry Williams was to become a good deal more than that, because his lawyer Cornelius J. Jones, Jr., like Blackburn Dovener twenty years before, intended to make his client the centerpiece of one of the most important voting rights cases ever brought before the United States Supreme Court.

The biggest difference in the two cases was that, unlike Dovener, Cornelius Jones was black.

To say it was rare for a black lawyer to induce dread among white Mississippi politicians in the 1890s is an understatement, but that is precisely what Cornelius Jones did. Tireless and without fear, by the time he took up Henry Williams's case, Jones had already spent more than five years on a crusade to overthrow the 1890 Mississippi constitution.

Jones was born in Vicksburg, Mississippi, in 1858, the son of two slaves who registered their marriage after the city had fallen to Ulysses Grant in July 1863. He attended a Freedmen's Bureau school—set up to provide an education to the children of freed slaves—and eventually enrolled at the newly commissioned Alcorn University. Alcorn's first president was an

African American, Hiram Revels, who resigned a seat in the United States Senate to accept the position.

After graduation, Jones worked briefly as a schoolteacher in Louisiana, then returned to Mississippi to study law. There he was hired by Anselm McLaurin, considered the foremost criminal lawyer in the state. McLaurin would later be elected governor, appointed as senator, and become one of the most important members of the state's 1890 constitutional convention. Although McLaurin was a most unlikely mentor for Cornelius Jones, this bastion of white supremacy was drawn to the young black lawyer.

In 1888, as he turned thirty, Jones decided to enter politics. Black voters, once a majority in Mississippi, had decreased in number but were still sufficiently represented that Jones won a seat in the state legislature. As soon as the voting provisions of the 1890 constitution went into effect, however, Jones was voted out of his seat. He almost immediately turned to the legal system to test the provisions of the Mississippi constitution that had denied him and his fellow black legislators their positions in government.

The first case he found was another ordinary murder, a workplace killing. On January 9, 1892, a black laborer named John Gibson killed the manager of the Refuge Plantation, Robert Stinson, in a dispute over docked wages. Gibson admitted to being drunk and seeking out and confronting his victim. What was odd about the case was that Gibson was unarmed and the plant manager had both a six-shooter and a heavy wooden staff. Facing Gibson down, Stinson beat him with the stick until Gibson collapsed into the dirt. But Gibson struggled forward. Stinson fired his revolver but the shots missed. Gibson succeeded in reaching the other man, and, during the ensuing struggle, four more shots were heard and Stinson crumpled to the ground, dead on the spot.

As with the Williams case, had Gibson been white, a clever defense attorney might well have persuaded jurors that the murder had been committed in self-defense. But as it was, after Gibson's capture, he was quickly indicted, tried, and sentenced to hang.

Cornelius Jones had not been Gibson's lawyer at trial but took over for his appeal and succeeded in winning a new trial. At that second trial, Jones laid the groundwork for an eventual appeal to federal court on Fourteenth Amendment grounds, specifically that Gibson had been denied due process because he had not been judged by a jury of his peers, meaning other African Americans, none of whom were on the jury rolls. In 1892, Mississippi had begun drawing jurors from those registered to vote after the 1890 constitution was adopted. Before that, seven thousand adult African American men had been eligible for jury service in Bolivar County, where the trial would take place. Since Gibson's crime had been committed

HON. CORNELIUS J. JONES,
Mississippi Leader Who is Now Contesting for His Seat in Congress,
from the Shoe String District of Mississippi.

Cornelius J. Jones, Jr.

before the 1892 change took effect, Jones claimed that the jury pool should have been summoned based on the earlier voting rolls. As it was, "the great prejudice prevailing against him among the white race" ensured Gibson's conviction and denied him the constitutional protections to which he was entitled.

But Jones's motion to void—quash—the indictment on Fourteenth Amendment grounds was denied. Gibson was again convicted and sentenced to hang.

By the time Jones filed another appeal, this one to remove the case to federal court, he was also representing another accused murderer, Charley Smith. Jones made a similar motion at Smith's trial, to have the case removed to federal court. This motion was denied as well. Although the case against Smith was not terribly strong—the prosecution could only prove that he had started a brawl in which another man had been shot and killed—he, too, was convicted and sentenced to be hanged. Jones appealed both Gibson's and Smith's convictions to the Mississippi supreme court, where, as expected, he lost. He then announced his intention to bring his appeal to the United States Supreme Court.

To press the action, Jones journeyed to Washington, where he teamed with another African American attorney, Emmanuel Hewlett, a well-connected law school graduate of Boston University. Jones took his appeal to the public as well as to the Court and became a frequent speaker at churches and to civic groups, as well as the subject of numerous articles in the press. A talk he gave at the Vermont Avenue Baptist Church was covered by the *Washington Evening Star*, at the time the capital's leading newspaper. The subject of the meeting, the *Star* noted, "was to lay before the colored people of the city the merits of the case of John Gibson and Charley Smith against the state of Mississippi . . . Much interest is being manifested in the case, not only by the colored people here, but throughout the south generally, as it involves the question of colored men serving on juries in the south."

"There is a practice prevailing in many of the courts of the south," Jones told his audience, "and especially the state of Mississippi, wherein negroes, in state courts, are uniformly excluded from jury service in the courts, however well qualified, and this exclusion is on account of their race and color. The exclusion is effected by state officers purposely and intentionally." Jones insisted this was a "gross violation" of the Fourteenth Amendment to the Constitution and expressed confidence the justices would agree with him. If they did, "it will revolutionize the present system of jury service in many states of the south."

Smith was argued on December 16, 1895, and *Gibson* two days later. African American newspapers could not contain their praise for a black lawyer from the South who might change history by pleading landmark cases to the highest court in the land. "Mr. Jones is a Mississippian by birth," the *Washington Bee* wrote, "and a man who enjoys the full confidence and respect of the citizens of his State, regardless of race or color. Having occupied many places of honor with great credit, we are also creditably informed that the judges of the courts of the State and members of the bar respect him for his manly bearing and knowledge of the law in the conduct of his cases."

For all the praise, however, Jones and Hewlett did not conduct *Gibson* or *Smith* well. With *Virginia v. Rives* as precedent, they should have realized that if they could not provide evidence that black potential jurors had been excluded *specifically* on racial grounds, there would be no federal jurisdiction. And such demonstrations had become increasingly difficult. White Southern legislators would no longer make the mistake that West Virginia had in *Strauder*. The only avenue that seemed open was the precedent set in *Yick Wo*, that the administration of laws that seemed race-neutral had been obviously and blatantly discriminatory.

But Emmanuel Hewlett, who wrote the brief in *Gibson*, did not cite *Yick Wo*. Even worse, he and Jones presented no evidence in either case that demonstrated intentional discrimination by Mississippi officials, only certified statements by the plaintiffs that the discrimination in jury selection had been present.

Decisions in both cases were reported out on April 16, 1896, and both were unanimous. In *Gibson*, Justice Harlan reiterated that laws must be applied equally to all citizens, regardless of race, but since Jones and Hewlett had not sought to invoke discriminatory application, he reverted to *Rives* rule, in which a state had to announce discrimination to trigger a Fourteenth Amendment violation. "Neither the constitution of Mississippi," he wrote, "nor the statutes of that State prescribe any rule . . . which is not equally applicable to all citizens of the United States and to all persons within the jurisdiction of the State without regard to race, color or previous condition of servitude." As such, he concluded, "We can do nothing but affirm the action of the [Mississippi supreme court] in denying this motion."

Gibson was thus denied, as was Smith in a similar ruling. Both were subsequently executed.

The following month, Harlan would break with his colleagues and cast the sole dissenting vote in *Plessy v. Ferguson*, the notorious "separate but equal" case. Harlan's ferocious defense of equal protection of law for all citizens is another of the most widely quoted opinions in American jurisprudence—although it had no effect on his fellow members of the Court. "In view of the constitution, in the eye of the law, there is in this country no superior, dominant, ruling class of citizens. There is no caste here. Our constitution is color-blind, and neither knows nor tolerates classes among citizens. In respect of civil rights, all citizens are equal before the law. The humblest is the peer of the most powerful. The law regards man as man, and takes no account of his surroundings or of his color when his civil rights as guaranteed by the supreme law of the land are involved."

One month after that, Henry Williams was convicted of murder and sentenced to death.

While taking up Williams's appeal, Cornelius Jones decided to run for Congress in Mississippi's third congressional district in the November 1896 election. His opponent was a six-term incumbent, Democrat Thomas Catchings, referred to in the newspapers as "General Catchings," even though he had served in the Confederate army only as a private. Jones did not expect to win, but, as with the Gibson and Smith cases, he intended to use the contest to mount a fresh assault on the 1890 constitution.

Catchings, as expected, received more than 80 percent of the votes, and soon afterward, Jones filed an official challenge. He claimed that the Mississippi constitution violated the United States Constitution. This was essentially the same charge that had been dismissed by the Supreme Court; this time the challenge would be judged by Congress. As was standard in such cases, Jones was awarded $2,000 to press his claim, which Mississippi newspapers insisted was his sole motivation. While Jones undoubtedly welcomed the money—it was a good deal more than he could make representing poor black criminal defendants—that he would raise the case at all greatly disturbed Mississippi whites.

Jones lost again, but the white political establishment in Mississippi had taken notice. They launched a series of personal attacks in state newspapers. In December 1896, for example, the *Greenville Times* wrote, "These experiences should have taught any head less thick than that of an African that he was wasting his time. If he had been conscientiously fighting for a principle he would no doubt have been convinced, but it is the double temptation of lucre and prestige with his race that actuates this chronic contestant."

Jones tried again in 1898, this time attempting to have ballots for Catchings disallowed on a technicality, claiming the ballots had been printed incorrectly. He lost once more and Thomas Catchings was again seated as the representative for Mississippi's third congressional district. Cornelius Jones did not run for Congress again.

Between his jousts with Mississippi Democrats for a congressional seat, Jones brought Henry Williams's appeal to the Supreme Court.

He had learned from the *Gibson* and *Smith* failures, and this time stressed that however the voting rights provisions of the Mississippi constitution were written, they were administered in a manner that denied black men access to the ballot box. Unfortunately, he could produce no statistics to back this up—none were available—relying on the obvious fact that more than 160,000 black voters had been stricken from the voting rolls since the new constitution was enacted.

On April 25, 1898, the Court issued its decision. The newest justice, Joseph McKenna, wrote the opinion. McKenna's legal credentials were so undistinguished that even his supporters were lukewarm. One of his advocates acknowledged

Joseph McKenna in front of shelves of law books.

that "he did not contend that Mr. McKenna was a giant in his legal attainments." McKenna had become so sensitive to charges during his confirmation hearings that he was, in fact, ignorant of many aspects of the law, that he had sat in on classes at Columbia University Law School before taking the bench.

Williams v. Mississippi was McKenna's first opinion and he began with the same high tone that characterized all equal rights decisions. "[The Fourteenth Amendment] and its effect upon the rights of the colored race have been considered by this Court in a number of cases, and it has been uniformly held that the Constitution of the United States, as amended, forbids, so far as civil and political rights are concerned, discriminations by the general government or by the states against any citizen because of his race."

Then McKenna set to deciding whether Mississippi voting laws had been administered in a discriminatory fashion. For most laymen, the answer would have been obvious. Almost none of its 907,000 black residents were eligible to go to the polls, and that included the 160,000 that had been registered before the new constitution became law. But rather than accept what a child could not have missed, Justice McKenna granted wide discretion to Mississippi's voting registrars—all of whom also were white. In the literacy test, if they chose a short simple phrase for whites—or even no phrase at all—and long, complex phrases for black citizens, the burden remained on Williams to *prove* that these choices had been made intentionally, on a *case-by-case basis*, to deny black people the right to register. And even if an individual officer had been shown to have discriminated, it was the fault of the man, not the constitution under which he was operating.

McKenna's opinion was dreadfully written and terribly racist, even by the standards of the day. He felt the need to include that the Mississippi supreme court had written that "the negro race had acquired or accentuated certain peculiarities of habit, of temperament, and of character which clearly distinguished it as a race apart from the whites; a patient, docile people, but careless, landless, migratory within narrow limits, without forethought, and its criminal members given to furtive offenses, rather than the robust crimes of the whites."

To sum up, McKenna wrote this final, incredible sentence: "The Constitution of Mississippi and its statutes do not on their face discriminate between the races, and it has not been shown that their actual administration was evil; only that evil was possible under them."

Jones's suit was denied. This vote was unanimous. Even Justice Harlan joined the majority. Henry Williams was executed.

Williams v. Mississippi was never overturned but remained legal precedent until passage of the Voting Rights Act of 1965.

Cornelius Jones never stopped fighting for the equal rights of his people. In 1915, he brought the first-ever attempt to gain reparations for the descendants of former slaves. He sued the United States Treasury for $68 million, the money they took in from taxes on cotton during the slavery era. The court of appeals in Washington, DC, dismissed the suit, saying the proper defendant was not the treasurer, but instead the United States government. And the United States government cannot be sued for damages by ordinary citizens. The Supreme Court upheld the decision.

CHAPTER 19

THE WINDOW SLAMS SHUT:
GILES V. HARRIS

O N MARCH 13, 1902, JACKSON W. Giles walked into the courthouse in Montgomery, Alabama, to once again register to vote. Giles, who worked as a janitor, had voted in Montgomery for more than twenty years, but like every other adult male, he had to reregister when Alabama enacted its new constitution in 1901. Giles's qualifications seemed excellent. He was employed, literate, owned his home, had no criminal record, and had paid his poll tax of $1.50.

But he was also black.

Although it had waited a decade, Alabama, like its brethren states, had drafted this new constitution specifically to remove Jackson Giles and more than 150,000 other African Americans from the voting rolls. As with the other states, there had been no trickery—Democrats had boasted of both their intent and their achievement. "We cannot afford to live with our feet upon fraud," exclaimed an Alabama Democrat in 1900. "We will not do it. We have disfranchised the African in the past by doubtful methods, but in the future we will do so by law." So proud were these white Alabamans in fashioning an electorate committed to "good government" and "traditional values" that they began their new constitution, with total seriousness, by mimicking the Declaration of Independence. "All men are equally free and independent; that they are endowed by their Creator with certain inalienable rights; that among these are life, liberty and the pursuit of happiness."

Even with *Williams v. Mississippi* on the books, Alabama Democrats knew that a legal test of their new constitution would come. As a result, neither of the two passages that discussed voter registration mentioned skin color. Section 180 granted permanent voting rights to any male over twenty-one years of age who registered before December 20, 1902, *and* was a veteran, or descendant of a veteran, of the Revolutionary War, the War of 1812, the Mexican War, the Indian Wars, the War between the States (on either side), or the Spanish-American War. This of course included virtually every white male in the state and only a handful of blacks. To make certain that those few whites whose ancestors hadn't fought anywhere would not be shut out, an additional category was included: "All persons who are of good character and who understand the duties and obligations of citizenship under a republican form of government." State officials would be able

Constitution of the State of Alabama.

1901.

We, the people of the State of Alabama, in order to establish justice, insure domestic tranquillity and secure the blessings of liberty to ourselves and our posterity, invoking the favor and guidance of Almighty God, do ordain and establish the following constitution and form of government for the State of Alabama:

Article 1.
Declaration of Rights.

That the great, general and essential principles of liberty and free government may be recognized and established, we declare:

1. That all men are equally free and independent; that they are endowed by their Creator with certain inalienable rights; that among these are life, liberty and the pursuit of happiness.

2. That all political power is inherent in the people, and all free governments are founded on their authority and instituted for their benefit; and that, therefore, they have at all times an inalienable and indefeasible right to change their form of government in such manner as they may deem expedient.

3. That no religion shall be established by law; that no preference shall be given by law to any religious sect, society, denomination or mode of worship; that no one shall be compelled by law to attend any place of worship; nor to pay any tithes, taxes or other rates for building or repairing any place of worship, or for maintaining any minister or ministry; that no religious test shall be required as a qualification to any office or public trust under this State; and that the civil rights, privileges and capacities of any citizen shall not be, in any manner, affected by his religious principles.

4. That no law shall ever be passed to curtail or restrain the liberty of speech or of the press; and any person may speak, write and publish his sentiments on all subjects, being responsible for the abuse of that liberty.

5. That the people shall be secure in their persons, houses, papers and possessions from unreasonable seizures or searches, and that no

1901 Alabama constitution, filled with lofty rhetoric.

to decide exactly who would meet that standard, and they made clear that just about all of them would be white. Voters qualified under Section 180 were required to pay a poll tax, but unless they were convicted of a felony, they would remain on the voting rolls for life.

Section 181 laid out the requirements for adult males who had not already registered by January 1, 1903, which took in just about every African American in the state. For these men, registration would not be permanent—they would need to reregister personally for each election in which they wished to vote. In addition to paid-up poll taxes, each would need to prove that he or his wife owned forty acres of land with paid-up property taxes of at least $300. Those who owned no property needed to be able to "read and write any article of the Constitution of the United States in the English language" and, unless "physically unable to work," had "worked or been regularly engaged in some lawful employment, business, or occupation, trade or calling, for the greater part of the twelve months next preceding the time they offer to register." Low-end workers were paid in cash, so whether or not to accept the word of a black man who claimed to have been employed was left to the discretion of the registrar.

With an eye to the court battle to come, Alabama registrars were careful not to shut out every black voter. Lifetime voting rights were granted to African American veterans of the army or navy who presented valid discharge papers, so tiny a percentage of the population that it would have no impact on state and local elections. Other prominent African Americans, such as Booker T. Washington, were also registered. As Governor William Dorsey Jelks noted, registrars "would carry out the spirit of the Constitution, which looks to the registration of all white men not convicted of crimes, and only a few Negroes." (Jelks was also widely known for his advocacy of lynching as an appropriate punishment for African Americans accused of attacking white women.)

Booker T. Washington in particular was handled with great care. Born a slave in 1856, he attended school after the Civil War and eventually the Hampton Normal and Agricultural Institute. Even as a young man, Washington was convinced that the proper road for black Americans was self-reliance and economic success, especially through business ownership. When he was just twenty-five, he became the principal of the newly founded Tuskegee School in rural Alabama, which would train young African American men and women to be teachers of the next generations, and "to return to the plantation districts and show the people there how to put new energy and new ideas into farming as well as into the intellectual and moral and religious life of the people."

A number of wealthy white Americans, such as John D. Rockefeller and Andrew Carnegie, found Washington's

Booker T. Washington.

message of self-reliance appealing and contributed both money and their personal prestige to the school. Tuskegee was able to expand—it is now Tuskegee University—and Booker T. Washington became a nationally known figure. That his followers were hardworking, honest, nonviolent, and acted within the law gave him more appeal in the white community than perhaps any other person of color in the nation.

But as Tuskegee prospered and its graduates attained at least limited success in a white world, conditions for people of color in the South were quickly becoming much worse. In addition to being denied the vote and the enjoyment of the basic rights of citizenship, African Americans were regularly beaten and jailed without cause, and hundreds were lynched. Washington, in his desire to prevent his people from being brutalized, proposed an extremely controversial solution.

In 1895, in a speech before a mostly white audience at the Cotton States and International Exposition in Atlanta, he endorsed segregation as a basis for cooperation between the races. In the "Atlanta Compromise," as it came to be known, Washington urged white Americans to encourage "ignorant and inexperienced" black citizens by offering them basic and simple job opportunities in agriculture and industry. From there perhaps, people of color could work their way into mainstream society. He also went on record as accepting voting restrictions based on literacy, education, or personal worth.

While white leaders praised Washington for offering a "realistic" solution to the race problems in America, many black leaders, such as W. E. B. Du Bois, were furious with him for selling out to oppression and ignoring the terrible abuses heaped on his people by the white citizenry. But Washington, by telling white people what they wanted to hear, became a showpiece and was even appointed as an advisor to President Theodore Roosevelt. Granting him a lifetime right to vote, it seemed to white Alabamans, would show the world they were willing to accept the "right" sort of Negro.

Jackson Giles was not Booker T. Washington, however, and so his application to register to vote was denied. But that did not surprise Jackson Giles at all. He had not only expected it, he had *planned* on it. In addition to his janitorial job, Jackson Giles was president of the Colored Men's Suffrage Association of Alabama, a group formed specifically to protest the voting rules of the 1901 Alabama constitution. He was at the Montgomery courthouse that March day to create grounds for a legal challenge that he and his backers intended to press on appeal all the way to the United States Supreme Court. In addition to his own claim, Giles would also represent five thousand other qualified African Americans similarly denied the right to register to vote.

When Jackson Giles began preparing his case for federal

court, he intended to present all the proof that Cornelius Jones in *Williams v. Mississippi* had not. He set to compiling reams of statistics, newspaper reports, and affidavits, all to demonstrate that, as in *Yick Wo*, a seemingly evenhanded law was being employed solely to discriminate against a specific class of individual, in this case black voters. It was an enormous task. To Giles's surprise, a prominent African American attorney from New York, Wilford H. Smith, suddenly volunteered to step in, supply the appropriate resources, and handle the case in court, all without a fee. A stunned but happy Jackson Giles gratefully accepted, unsure how his case had become known to an attorney in New York.

But Wilford Smith was not just any attorney in New York. He was Booker T. Washington's personal lawyer. Unbeknownst to both Giles and those he intended to sue, Smith had been hired, with great secrecy, by the very same man that white Alabamans had tried so hard to bring on their side, the very same man other black leaders accused of being a sellout.

Washington was aware that his ability to have any influence at all depended on white people believing he accepted both segregation and the phony restrictions Southerners had placed on African American voting. To hide his true intentions, he directed that all correspondence between him and Wilford Smith be handled by his private secretary, Emmett

J. Scott. They used code names for important messages, with Washington himself at first referred to with a series of false names, like "Filipino," "His Nibs," or "the Wizard." When Washington realized that anyone reading the letters would know immediately to whom those names referred, Scott switched to aliases like R. C. Black (for himself) and J. C. May (for Smith) and left out references to Washington altogether.

Giles and Smith eventually brought suit against E. Jeff Harris and the other members of the Board of Registrars of Montgomery County. They lost in state court and in federal district court, as they expected, and on February 24, 1903, *Giles v. Harris* reached the Supreme Court. Wilford Smith presented overwhelming evidence to the justices that the discrimination against his client sprang directly from the 1901 Alabama constitution—no matter how evenhandedly it pretended to be worded—and therefore met all the requirements the Court had established to strike down a law as a violation of the Fourteenth and Fifteenth Amendments. His documentation was so persuasive that the attorneys for Alabama could do little to contest it.

The Court had undergone an important change since *Williams*. In 1902, President Theodore Roosevelt had appointed to the high bench a man of towering reputation, a celebrated legal philosopher and former war hero, a man destined to become almost as famous as the court on which he served.

Oliver Wendell Holmes, Jr., was born in Boston in March 1841. His father, Oliver Wendell Holmes, Sr., was a famed physician, as well as a sparkling writer, poet, and philosopher. He was known for rational thinking and deductive reasoning—working from evidence to reach a conclusion—and is generally thought to have lent his name to Arthur Conan Doyle, when Doyle was considering writing stories about a fictional detective whose first name was "Sherlock." At age thirty, Holmes, Sr., married a noted abolitionist, Amelia Lee Jackson.

It is rare that a son could outshine such a famed and celebrated father, but Holmes, Jr., did. After fighting in some of the most famous battles of the Civil War, including Chancellorsville, Fredericksburg, and Antietam—and being wounded three times—Holmes left the army and studied law at Harvard. (His father had studied law as well but had never practiced.) While working as an attorney for fifteen years, Holmes wrote articles about the philosophy of law, some of which were published in a book that is still read by law students more than 125 years later. He served on the Massachusetts supreme judicial court, as both associate and chief justice, and all the while his reputation soared. His successor on the Supreme Court, Benjamin Cardozo, praised him as "probably the greatest legal intellect in the history of the English-speaking world."

Holmes would serve on the Supreme Court for thirty years and, after his death in 1935, would be acclaimed in a bestselling biography, *Yankee from Olympus*, and become the subject of an Oscar-nominated film, *The Magnificent Yankee* (Louis Calhern lost for Best Actor to José Ferrer playing Cyrano de Bergerac). In another Oscar-winning film, *Judgment at Nuremberg*, Holmes would be portrayed as the personification of American fairness.

To this day, Oliver Wendell Holmes, Jr., is widely thought of as a great champion of civil liberties and an unwavering defender of democratic ideals.

If that was the Oliver Wendell Holmes who sat as an associate justice of the Supreme Court, he, along with Jackson Giles, Wilford Smith, and Booker T. Washington, might have changed the course of American history.

But Holmes was far more complex than either Hollywood, flattering biographers, or even fellow justices portrayed. He was a committed Social Darwinist who believed in the superiority of the white race, and in religion his views were equally intolerant. In 1916, when Louis Brandeis was finally confirmed as an associate justice after a bitter floor fight in the Senate—the notion of a Jew on the Court disgusted many senators—Holmes observed that he would rather "see power in the hands of the Jews than the Catholics," although he

Oliver Wendell Holmes, Jr.

really did not "want to be run by either." In 1927, he would write the notorious opinion in *Buck v. Bell*, which upheld the forced sterilization of a nineteen-year-old woman judged— incorrectly, as it turned out—to be intellectually disabled. "Three generations of imbeciles is enough," he wrote. Holmes was so obsessed with his image that, shortly before his death, he destroyed any personal papers that might reflect poorly on his reputation, retaining only those that painted him in a favorable light.

This was the Oliver Wendell Holmes that Jackson Giles was up against.

Holmes had taken his seat in December 8, 1902, and *Giles v. Harris* would be his first major case. Morrison Waite had died in 1888 and his successor as chief justice, Melville Fuller, chose Holmes to write the opinion. On April 27, 1903, the case was decided. The vote was 6–3.

Holmes's opinion was brief, only six pages. Bowing to the weight of Wilford Smith's evidence, Holmes agreed that the voting rights provisions of the Alabama constitution did indeed discriminate against the state's black citizens. This was just the sort of case, then, that even Joseph Bradley and Morrison Waite would have seen as a violation of the Fifteenth Amendment. It would have been reasonable from there to assume that the Court would be ruling for Giles and the five thousand African American plaintiffs.

But neither the Supreme Court of the United States nor Oliver Wendell Holmes personally had any intention of compelling Southern states to grant black citizens the right to vote, no matter what the Fifteenth Amendment said. In the last two pages of the opinion, Holmes denied Giles's claim, but what was more significant were the ridiculous lengths to which he was forced to go to justify his opinion. Holmes's reasoning was such a distortion of constitutional principles that legal scholar Richard Pildes called *Giles v. Harris* the "one key moment, one decisive turning point . . . in the bleak and unfamiliar saga . . . of the history of anti-democracy in the United States."

To begin with, Holmes claimed that since Giles insisted "the whole registration scheme of the Alabama Constitution is a fraud upon the Constitution of the United States, and asks us to declare it void," Giles was suing "to be registered as a party qualified under the void instrument." If the Court then ruled in Giles's favor, Holmes concluded, it would become "a party to the unlawful scheme by accepting it and adding another voter to its fraudulent lists."

By this definition, *any* law that was discriminatory would be a "fraud," and the Court would become party to that fraud by protecting the plaintiff's right as a citizen. It would follow that the Supreme Court could not ever protect *any* citizen from *any* state law, which was precisely what the Fourteenth and Fifteenth Amendments said the Court *must* do. Even using Joseph Bradley's strangled view of the Fifteenth Amendment, here it was clear, as Holmes had admitted, that "citizens of the United States" were being denied the right to vote in Alabama "on account of race, color, or previous condition of servitude."

Holmes carefully avoided commenting on Smith's main point, that the two offending sections were discriminatory in their administration. If he had chosen to, Holmes could simply have declared Sections 180 and 181 void, and that any state provision that, in word or application, prevented equal access to the ballot box would also be void. There was ample precedent in previous cases to strike down only one section of a law, but Holmes did not mention that alternative at all.

Holmes's second objection was that the Court "cannot undertake . . . to enforce political rights." "Political rights" is one of those hazy concepts in law whose definition changes depending on who is doing the defining. For example, if a state legislature gerrymanders congressional districts—shapes them in a distorted way to ensure that one party gets the lion's share of seats and the other party gets a lot fewer—is that a "political right" or a violation of equal protection of the laws and the rule of "one-man-one-vote"? The Court has ruled on each side of the issue at different points in history. The Court's role in enforcing—or not enforcing—"political rights" with respect to African Americans has been a particular source of debate. But whatever position one takes on whether or not the Court should ensure political rights, Holmes's reasoning was tortured and again rather ridiculous.

He began by observing that since "the great mass of the white population intends to keep the blacks from voting . . .

something more than ordering the plaintiff's name to be inscribed upon the lists of 1902 will be needed." That "something" would be federal intervention. "Unless we are prepared to supervise the voting in that state by officers of the court, it seems to us that all that the plaintiff could get from [a favorable decision] would be an empty form." In other words, since the Court could not enforce its ruling, it should make no ruling at all.

But the Court has no power of enforcement for *any* ruling. It has no dedicated police force, no power over Congress. The Court gains its authority *only* from the willingness of the parties to adhere to its rulings and to the Constitution. If one of the parties refuses, force of arms, a tool of the other branches of government, may be used to ensure compliance. (As was the case sixty years later, when the government used federal troops and marshals to enforce school integration and the 1965 Voting Rights Act.)

So Jackson Giles lost and the Alabama constitution was approved by the highest court in the land.

Holmes's opinion in *Giles* cut away the last hope American citizens of color had to be able to have a voice in their government in the South. Previous court decisions had limited the reach of the Fourteenth and Fifteenth Amendments with respect to African Americans to actions by a state, and then further restricted the amendments to actual state laws, rather than the actions of state employees. Now, it seemed, even state laws acknowledged to be discriminatory would be allowed to stand.

Most sad is that *Giles v. Harris* was in no way an exception in the Supreme Court's commitment to allowing—even encouraging—voting rolls, especially but not exclusively in the South, to remain white. Rather, the decision was remarkable precisely because it was so unremarkable.

EPILOGUE

STOLEN JUSTICE

THERE IS NO MORE VITAL right in a democracy than the right to vote. Without it, no other right is secure.

By permitting Southern states to rob African Americans of that right, the nine justices of the Supreme Court allowed—or, more accurately, encouraged—America to become the land of slavery in all but name, to permit the oppression of United States citizens as if they were still just property. In decision after decision, the Court chose to allow white supremacists to re-create a social order at odds with legislation that Congress had passed, the president had signed, and the states had ratified. Always claiming strict adherence to the language of the law, they ruled time and again to deny fundamental rights to black Americans. Yet the Court did not render its decisions to conform to the law, but instead twisted the law to conform to its decisions.

Rather than being the guardian of the rights of ordinary people, as Alexander Hamilton had assured Americans it would be, the Court opted to grant rights to some while taking them away from others. All men, it seemed, were not created equal after all. The justices did not rule on the spirit of the law; instead they chose to support—and reinforce—the distaste expressed by white Americans to share their freedoms with people of color. In a series of decisions spanning three decades, the Supreme Court of the United States announced that it considered popular sentiment and its own notions of racial superiority more important than the promise of equality under the Constitution.

In order to do so, the justices were forced to ignore—or pretend to ignore—the horrific acts of violence and abuse suffered by African Americans because their rights had been denied by the very Supreme Court on which they sat. While the justices debated the meaning of this clause or that, they did not seem to notice that in the nation of which they were the highest authority on what the law meant and how it was administered, men, women, and children were being slaughtered. Between 1890 and 1903, 1,889 lynchings were conducted in the United States. In 1,405 of those cases, the victims were black. According to records compiled by Booker T. Washington's Tuskegee Institute, 70 to 80 percent of those lynchings occurred in the South.

By 1904, each of the eleven states that had formed the Confederacy had instituted a poll tax, most in combination with a grandfather clause, and seven had demanded literacy tests. Poll taxes were generally assessed on a running total, so virtually no black applicant could pay. As the South sunk into one-party rule, laws mandating white primaries—meaning only white voters could participate in the elections that chose who would run for office—became widespread, so votes in general elections by the few African Americans who had slipped through the net were certain to be meaningless. By 1906, 83 percent of white males in the South were registered to vote, compared to 2 percent of black men.

With voting rights denied, Southern state governments proceeded to segregate virtually every aspect of public life. In 1905, Georgia passed a law forbidding African Americans from entering public parks and within a few years, people of color were excluded from virtually all park facilities throughout the South. Forced segregation was soon mandated at factory entrances, pay windows, movie theaters, restaurants, on streetcars and railroads, in grocery stores, taverns, and, especially, schools, cemeteries, and public toilets. By 1910, African Americans had been effectively herded out of the white South into decrepit, slum-ridden ghettos called "Darktowns." To postulate that the Jim Crow restrictions were intended to be as severe as the restrictions put on slaves would not be an exaggeration.

The right to vote has always been viewed as the one great privilege and the one great responsibility of American democracy. But those who wished to exercise that right have often had to fight to achieve it; incredibly brave men and women who risked their lives to pierce the soul of the nation and end the denial of voting rights for African Americans and the racial segregation that flowed from this fundamental inequity.

On March 7, 1965, a group of six hundred of those men and women, led by John Lewis, now a long-serving Georgia congressman, and Hosea Williams, of the Southern Christian Leadership Conference, set out from a church in Selma, Alabama, on a planned fifty-four-mile march to Montgomery, the state capital. Lewis was only twenty-five years old, the son of an Alabama sharecropper and the chairman of the Student Nonviolent Coordinating Committee, an organization dedicated to ending segregation and ensuring access of his fellow African Americans to the ballot box. In Selma, only about three hundred of the more than fifteen thousand eligible black voters had been allowed to actually register.

When the marchers reached the Edmund Pettus Bridge, which spanned the Alabama River and had been named for a Confederate general who had also been a grand dragon of the Alabama Ku Klux Klan, they saw dozens of white-helmeted state troopers waiting for them on the other side. The troopers were slapping nightsticks in their hands, warning the marchers not to try to cross. Whips and tear gas canisters hung from their belts. The Dallas County sheriff, Jim Clark, and his deputies, some on horseback, waited behind them. Dozens of jeering white spectators waving Confederate flags were on the scene as well.

John Lewis and the other leaders of the march were determined that the protest be nonviolent. They instructed the marchers not to fight back if attacked.

And attacked they were. Viciously and with the fury of hate. Lewis and his fellow marchers were teargassed, beaten with nightsticks—Lewis suffered a fractured skull—whipped, and run down by horses. Many troopers and attackers spat on the injured marchers as they lay helpless on the ground. All because they were trying to obtain their constitutionally guaranteed right to vote.

There had been many such incidents of white brutality across the South, but this one was filmed by newsmen for the entire world to see. On the ABC network, the television premiere of the movie *Judgment at Nuremberg*, about the trials of Nazi war criminals, was interrupted so that millions could witness for themselves the horrible violence in Selma. The incident was soon dubbed "Bloody Sunday," and within days, demonstrations against Southern racism were held in more than eighty United States cities.

And finally, after decades of denial, the government acted. On March 15, President Lyndon Johnson appeared before a

John Lewis clubbed by an Alabama state trooper, who fractured Lewis's skull in the attack.

special joint session of Congress and told the assembled senators and representatives:

> The harsh fact is that in many places in this country men and women are kept from voting simply because they are Negroes. Every device of which human ingenuity is capable has been used to deny this right. The Negro citizen may go to register only to be told that the day is wrong, or the hour is late, or the official in charge is absent. And if he persists, and if he manages to present himself to the registrar, he may be disqualified because he did not spell out his middle name or because he abbreviated a word on the application.
>
> And if he manages to fill out an application he is given a test. The registrar is the sole judge of whether he passes this test. He may be asked to recite the entire Constitution, or explain the most complex provisions of state law. And even a college degree cannot be used to prove that he can read and write. For the fact is that the only way to pass these barriers is to show a white skin . . .
>
> What happened in Selma is part of a far larger movement which reaches into every section and State of America. It is the effort of American Negroes to secure for themselves the

President Lyndon B. Johnson addresses Congress on March 15, 1965, in a special joint session.

full blessings of American life. Their cause must be our cause too. Because it is not just Negroes, but really it is all of us, who must overcome the crippling legacy of bigotry and injustice.

And we *shall* overcome.

Two days after the president spoke, the Senate majority leader, Democrat Mike Mansfield, and the minority leader, Republican Everett Dirksen, together introduced a bill to guarantee voting rights to African Americans. A similar bill was soon introduced in the House of Representatives. Over the ferocious opposition of Southern congressmen, the bill passed in both houses and, on August 6, 1965, President Johnson signed the Voting Rights Act into law.

The 1965 Voting Rights Act has been widely considered the single most effective piece of civil rights legislation ever produced in the United States. The law banned literacy tests and many other of the contrivances used in Southern states to deny the vote to men and women of color. Harking back to the Enforcement Acts of the 1870s, it allowed the federal government to send election supervisors to any state or county where discriminatory practices existed as of the 1964 presidential election, or where voter turnout or registration for that election had fallen below 50 percent of the voting age population. These were called "special coverage areas," and in these locations, local and state governments would be required to gain permission from the federal government before making any change to their election laws or voting procedures.

The law was an enormous and immediate success. In Selma, eight days after President Johnson signed the bill into law, federal officials helped 381 African Americans to register to vote, more than had been able to sign up in Dallas County for *sixty-five years*. By Election Day 1965, eight thousand new black voters helped turn Sheriff Clark out of office and into a mobile home salesman. African American voter registration exploded in every state that had been a part of the old Confederacy, nowhere more than in Mississippi, where in

March 1965, only 6.7 percent of eligible African Americans had been registered. By November 1988, that number had jumped to 74.2 percent.

With increased participation in the electoral process, men and women of color were once more elected to public office, and now represent the nation in both the Senate and the House of Representatives, and by the hundreds in state and local offices. After more than a century, the promise of Reconstruction had begun to be kept.

But that promise may turn out to be as elusive now as it was before. On June 25, 2013, the Supreme Court, in a 5–4 decision, ruled in *Shelby County, Alabama v. Holder*, that the formula for determining which states and localities would be designated "special coverage areas" was unconstitutional, because after almost fifty years, conditions had improved so much that the formula no longer represented reality. Unless the federal government could demonstrate that these rules were still required, wrote Chief Justice John Roberts in his majority opinion, which was joined by Justices Scalia, Thomas, Kennedy, and Alito, it was a violation of the rights of states and localities to require them to get permission before they could change their election laws. "Our country has changed," Chief Justice Roberts wrote. "While any racial discrimination in voting is too much, Congress must ensure that the legislation it passes to remedy that problem speaks to current conditions."

Justice Ruth Bader Ginsburg wrote a strong dissent, in which she was joined by Justices Breyer, Kagan, and Sotomayor. She agreed that racial discrimination at the ballot box in the states that still required pre-clearance had decreased, but that was precisely because the law had remained in place. "Throwing out pre-clearance when it has worked and is continuing to work to stop discriminatory changes," she argued "is like throwing away your umbrella in a rainstorm because you are not getting wet."

If the requirement was eliminated, the dissenters predicted, discrimination might well begin again. And so it has. According to the Brennan Center for Justice, "The decision in *Shelby County* opened the floodgates to laws restricting voting throughout the United States. The effects were immediate. Within 24 hours of the ruling, Texas announced that it would implement a strict photo ID law. Two other states, Mississippi and Alabama, also began to enforce photo ID laws that had previously been barred because of federal preclearance."

Other states have followed suit. In Georgia, for example, in July 2017, 600,000 people, 8 percent of the state's registered voters, were purged from the rolls and required to reregister—an estimated 107,000 of them simply because they hadn't voted in recent elections. In 2018, the state blocked the registration of 53,000 state residents, 70 percent of whom were African American.

Voter ID laws and other restrictions that fall heaviest on African American, Latinx, and poor people have been initiated in a number of other states, not all in the South. Polling locations have been closed, early voting restricted, and registration rules made stricter, all, critics insist, to suppress the vote of certain classes and races. In some states, the same sort of "exact match" rules that President Johnson cited in his speech to Congress have been reinstituted.

And so, what Americans should never forget is that the right to vote should never be taken for granted, never assumed to be "just there," because it is never "just there." Remaining a nation that truly values freedom and justice requires that all Americans insist that their fellow citizens, no matter what their race, gender, religion, or political belief, be allowed to participate in choosing the nation's leaders.

That simple principle remains a challenge for us all.

GLOSSARY

Amendment: An addition to the Constitution that either clarified a passage that had not been precise, changed the powers of the federal government—usually by expanding them—or limited the power of the states to enact certain types of laws.

Appeal: An attempt to retry a case in a higher court after an unfavorable verdict.

Appellate jurisdiction: A court that has the power to hear appeals of a verdict given in a different court.

Bill of Rights: The first ten amendments to the Constitution, adopted by the 1st Congress. Most amendments laid out rights of individuals or how the federal government could or could not limit those rights. The Tenth Amendment limited the powers of the federal government with respect to state governments.

Black Codes: Laws passed after the Civil War by white-dominated governments of former Confederate states that denied African Americans basic rights of citizenship.

***Brown v. Board of Education*:** A 1954 Supreme Court case in which a unanimous verdict stated that racial segregation in public schools was forbidden by the Constitution. It did not address segregation in any other area.

Canvassing board: A group of people appointed to examine voting records and determine whether or not the reported totals were correct.

Carpetbagger: A Northerner who came south after the Civil War. Many Southerners accused these people of caring only about making money or gaining power in the defeated Confederacy, while others believed most came to help integrate the freed slaves into mainstream society.

Chinese Exclusion Act: A law passed in 1882 forbidding all Chinese laborers from entering the United States, the first law in United States history aimed at preventing immigration by a specific racial or ethnic group.

Circuit court: The middle layer of the federal judiciary. Circuit courts are mostly appellate, ruling on cases in which the loser in district court seeks a different ruling.

Civil Rights Act of 1875: The first federal law ever to guarantee people of any race equal access to public accommodations, such as restaurants, hotels, theaters, and parks, as well as means of public transportation. It also forbade denying anyone service on a jury because of race.

Defendant: Someone accused of a crime or misdeed.

Democratic Party: Originally a "states' rights" political party, begun by Andrew Jackson after his loss in the presidential election of 1824, in which he got more popular and electoral votes than either of his opponents.

District court: The lowest layer of the federal court system. District courts take any case in which a plaintiff can demonstrate that the action comes under federal law.

Dred Scott v. Sandford: An 1857 Supreme Court decision that returned an African American to slavery even though he had been brought to a free state. It declared that anyone whose ancestors had been brought to the United States as slaves could never be an American citizen.

Emancipation Proclamation: The January 1, 1863, order by President Abraham Lincoln that freed slaves in all areas controlled by the Confederacy. The order did not apply to slave states that had remained in the Union—Maryland, Delaware, Missouri, and Kentucky—nor to areas under Union control, such as Tennessee and New Orleans.

Enforcement Acts: Laws passed by Congress during Reconstruction to ensure that the provisions of the Fourteenth and Fifteenth Amendments were adhered to in the conquered South.

Freedmen: Freed slaves.

Fusionists: A political party or movement that was a blend of other parties that had previously been adversaries.

Grand jury: A panel of citizens whose role it is to decide if there is enough evidence to indict—bring to trial—someone accused of a crime.

Grandfather clause: A rule that automatically grants the right to vote to any eligible person, usually male, whose father or grandfather was also a registered voter. These were used extensively to deny the vote to freedmen, whose fathers and grandfathers were slaves and could not vote. Grandfather clauses to restrict voting rights were ruled unconstitutional by the Supreme Court in 1915.

Indictment: An official accusation issued by a grand jury or a judge to bring to trial a person or persons said to have committed a crime.

Judicial review: The power of a federal court to declare a law unconstitutional. The final decision on constitutionality will almost always be made by the Supreme Court.

Judiciary: A system of courts.

Naturalization Act: A law that sets conditions under which an immigrant can become an American citizen. There was a series of such laws in the first decades after American independence, and others since, as recently as 1990.

Page Act: An 1875 law, sponsored by Congressman Horace Page, that barred certain Chinese laborers and many Chinese women from entering the United States.

Paramilitary: Civilians operating as if they were soldiers.

Petit jury (or simply "jury"): A panel that decides whether the plaintiff or defendant wins, often the guilt or innocence of the defendant.

Plaintiff: The party bringing a lawsuit or making an accusation.

Plessy v. Ferguson: An 1896 Supreme Court decision that made segregation of whites and African Americans legal, as long as the facilities available to each group were equal.

Poll tax: A payment required to enable a person to vote. In 1964, the Twenty-Fourth Amendment to the Constitution made poll taxes illegal in all national elections, and two years later the Supreme Court ruled poll taxes illegal in state elections.

Polygenism: A discarded scientific theory that claimed different races descended from different ancestors, making black people and Asians not really "human" in the same sense as white people.

Radical Republicans: Congressmen after the Civil War who insisted that the United States accept freed slaves fully and completely as citizens, and punish anyone in the former Confederacy who opposed that aim.

Ratification: Agreement to adopt a document or plan, usually by vote.

Reconstruction: A program to integrate freed slaves into ordinary society and to protect their rights as citizens. An important part of Reconstruction was to specify the conditions under which Confederate states could rejoin the Union.

Reconstruction Acts: Laws passed by Congress to set those conditions and also to ensure that states in the old Confederacy did not abuse the rights of their new black citizens. One of the acts divided the Confederacy into five military districts, each under the command of an army general.

Red Shirts: A paramilitary Redeemer group formed in North Carolina to take back control of state and local governments by force.

Redeemer: Someone who, after the Civil War, wanted to return the South to the same social structure as before the war. African Americans could no longer be called slaves, but they would be treated in the "Redeemed" South as if they still were. Some Redeemer groups turned to violence, such as the "Kuklux," later the Ku Klux Klan, and the Order of the White Camellia.

Republican Party: A political party formed in the 1850s to oppose the expansion of slavery. Their first candidate for president was Abraham Lincoln in 1860.

Social Darwinism: A now discredited theory that people or classes of people who are more successful in society are inherently superior to those who are not.

Suffragette: A woman campaigning for women's right to vote.

Supreme Court: The highest court in the United States, the top layer of the federal judiciary. The Supreme Court consists of a chief justice and associate justices, since 1869, fixed at eight. The Supreme Court's jurisdiction is almost exclusively appellate, although there are some rare instances when cases will begin there, called "original jurisdiction."

Tammany Hall: A Democratic Party organization that wielded enormous political power in New York City and New York State in the late nineteenth and early twentieth centuries. Leaders of Tammany Hall, especially William Magear "Boss" Tweed, combined loyalty from immigrants and working people with bribery and election fraud to control much of city politics.

Trial: A court proceeding in which a decision is reached that favors either the plaintiff or the defendant. In some cases, in a "mistrial" or a "hung jury," no decision is reached and the trial must be conducted again.

Verdict: A decision in a court case. A verdict can be rendered, or announced, by a jury, a judge, or sometimes a panel of judges.

BIBLIOGRAPHY

ONLINE RESOURCES

Congressional Globe. https://memory.loc.gov/ammem/amlaw/lwcg.html
Statutes at Large. https://www.loc.gov/law/help/statutes-at-large/index.php
United States Reports. https://www.loc.gov/collections/united-states-reports/
http://www.lbjlibrary.org/lyndon-baines-johnson/speeches-films/president-johnsons-special-message-to-the-congress-the-american-promise
https://supreme.justia.com/cases/federal/us/570/12-96/#tab-opinion-1970752
https://epic.org/privacy/voting/register/intro_c.html
https://www.brennancenter.org/analysis/effects-shelby-county-v-holder

BOOKS AND ARTICLES

"The Alabama Franchise Case." *Harvard Law Review*, Vol. 17, No. 2 (December 1903).

"Anselm J. McLaurin (late a senator from Mississippi)." United States Government printing office, 1911.

"Congressional Power under the Civil War Amendments." *Duke Law Journal*, Vol. 1969, No. 6 (December 1969).

"Constitutionality of the Grandfather Clauses." *Columbia Law Review*, Vol. 14, No. 4 (April 1914).

"The Strange Career of 'State Action' under the Fifteenth Amendment." *Yale Law Journal*, Vol. 74, No. 8 (July 1965), pp. 1448–1461.

Abraham, Harry J. "John Marshall Harlan: A Justice Neglected." *Virginia Law Review*, Vol. 41, No. 7 (November 1955).

Aichele, Gary J. *Oliver Wendell Holmes, Jr.: Soldier, Scholar, Judge*. Boston: Twayne Publishing, 1989.

Alschuler, Albert W. *Law without Values: The Life, Work, and Legacy of Justice Holmes*. Chicago: University of Chicago Press, 2000.

B. E. H. and J. J. K., Jr. "Federal Protection of Negro Voting Rights." *Virginia Law Review*, Vol. 51, No. 6 (October 1965).

Benedict, Michael Les. "Preserving Federalism: Reconstruction and the Waite Court." *Supreme Court Review*, Vol. 1978 (1978).

Bernstein, David E. "Revisiting *Yick Wo v. Hopkins*." *University of Illinois Law Review*, forthcoming; George Mason Law & Economics Research Paper No. 08-55 (September 2008).

Borchard, Edwin. "The Supreme Court and Private Rights." *Yale Law Journal*, Vol. 47, No. 7 (May 1938).

Brenner, Samuel. "'Airbrushed Out of the Constitutional Canon': The Evolving Understanding of *Giles v. Harris*, 1903–1925." *Michigan Law Review*, Vol. 107, No. 5 (March 2009).

Bruce, Philip Alexander. *History of the University of Virginia, 1819–1919*. Vol. 3, *The Lengthened Shadow of One Man*. New York: Macmillan Company, c. 1920–1922.

Champagne, Anthony, and Dennis Pope. "Joseph P. Bradley: An Aspect of a Judicial Personality." *Political Psychology*, Vol. 6, No. 3 (September 1985).

Chin, Gabriel J. "Unexplainable on Grounds of Race. Doubts about *Yick Wo*." *University of Illinois Law Review*, Vol. 2008 (August 2008).

Chin, Gabriel J., and Randy Wagner. "The Tyranny of the Minority: Jim Crow and the Counter-Majoritarian Difficulty." *Harvard Civil Rights-Civil Liberties Law Review*, Vol. 43 (2008).

Clarke, James W. "Without Fear or Shame: Lynching, Capital Punishment and the Subculture of Violence in the American South." *British Journal of Political Science*, Vol. 28, No. 2 (April 1998).

Corwin, Edward S. "The Supreme Court and the Fourteenth Amendment." *Michigan Law Review*, Vol. 7, No. 8 (June 1909).

Du Bois, W. E. B. *The Autobiography of W. E. B. Dubois: A Soliloquy on Viewing My Life from the Last Decade of Its First Century*. New York: International Publishers, 1968.

_____. "Reconstruction and Its Benefits." *American Historical Review*, Vol. 15, No. 4 (July 1910).

_____. "Reconstruction, Seventy-Five Years After." *Phylon*, Vol. 4, No. 3 (3rd Quarter 1943).

Epps, Garrett. *Democracy Reborn: The Fourteenth Amendment and the Fight for Equal Rights in Post–Civil War America*. New York: Henry Holt, 2006.

Field, Henry M., M.D. *Blood Is Thicker Than Water: A Few Days among Our Southern Brethren.* New York: George Munro, 1886.

Foner, Eric. *Freedom's Lawmakers: A Directory of Black Officeholders during Reconstruction,* rev. ed. Baton Rouge: Louisiana State University Press, 1996.

———. *Reconstruction: America's Unfinished Revolution, 1863–1877.* New York: Harper and Row, 1988.

———. "Reconstruction Revisited." *Reviews in American History,* Vol. 10, No. 4, The Promise of American History: Progress and Prospects (December 1982).

Franklin, John Hope. *Race and History: Selected Essays 1938–1988.* Baton Rouge: Louisiana State University Press, 1989.

———. "'Legal' Disfranchisement of the Negro." *Journal of Negro Education,* Vol. 26, No. 3, The Negro Voter in the South (Summer 1957).

Garner, James Wilford. *Reconstruction in Mississippi.* New York: Macmillan Company, 1901.

Graham, Howard Jay. "The 'Conspiracy Theory' of the Fourteenth Amendment." *Yale Law Journal,* Vol. 47, No. 3 (January 1938). And "The 'Conspiracy Theory' of the Fourteenth Amendment: 2." Vol. 48, No. 2 (December 1938).

Haller, John S., Jr. "The Species Problem: Nineteenth-Century Concepts of Racial Inferiority in the Origin of Man Controversy." *American Anthropologist,* New Series, Vol. 72, No. 6 (December 1970).

Hamm, Walter C. "The Three Phases of Colored Suffrage." *North American Review,* Vol. 168 (March 1899).

Harlan, Louis R. "The Secret Life of Booker T. Washington." *Journal of Southern History,* Vol. 37, No. 3 (August 1971).

H. M. J. "Federal Jurisdiction: The Civil Rights Removal Statute Revisited." *Duke Law Journal,* Vol. 1967, No. 1 (February 1967).

Hoeveler, J. David, Jr. "Reconstruction and the Federal Courts: The Civil Rights Act of 1875." *Historian,* Vol. 31, No. 4 (August 1969).

Hofstadter, Richard. *Social Darwinism in American Thought.* Boston: Beacon Press, 1959.

Horan, Michael J. "Political Economy and Sociological Theory as Influences upon Judicial Policy-Making: The Civil Rights Cases of 1883." *American Journal of Legal History,* Vol. 16, No. 1 (January 1972).

Hunt, Gaillard, ed. *The Writings of James Madison.* Vol. 9. New York: J. P. Putnam's and Sons, 1910.

Jones, Thomas Jesse. "Negro Population in the United States." *Annals of the American Academy of Political and Social Science,* Vol. 49, The Negro's Progress in Fifty Years (September 1913).

Keyssar, Alexander. *The Right to Vote: The Contested History of Democracy in the United States.* New York: Basic Books, 2000.

Klarman, Michael J. *From Jim Crow to Civil Rights: The Supreme Court and the Struggle for Racial Equality.* New York: Oxford University Press, 2004.

Kousser, J. Morgan. "Response to Commentaries." *Social Science History,* Vol. 24, No. 2 (Summer 2000).

———. *The Shaping of Southern Politics: Suffrage Restriction and the Establishment of the One-Party South, 1880–1910.* New Haven: Yale University Press, 1974.

———. *Colorblind Injustice: Minority Voting Rights and the Undoing of the Second Reconstruction.* Chapel Hill: University of North Carolina Press, 1999.

Kutler, Stanley I. "Reconstruction and the Supreme Court: The Numbers Game Reconsidered." *Journal of Southern History,* Vol. 32, No. 1 (February 1966).

———. *Judicial Power and Reconstruction Politics.* Chicago: University of Chicago Press, 1968.

Lane, Charles. *The Day Freedom Died: The Colfax Massacre, the Supreme Court, and the Betrayal of Reconstruction.* New York: Henry Holt & Company, 2008.

Levy, Leonard W. *Original Intent and the Framers' Constitution.* New York: Macmillan, 1988.

Lewis, Earl M. "The Negro Voter in Mississippi." *Journal of Negro Education,* Vol. 26, No. 3, The Negro Voter in the South (Summer 1957).

Litwack, Leon F. *Trouble in Mind: Black Southerners in the Age of Jim Crow.* New York: Alfred A. Knopf, 1998.

Lynd, Staughton. "Rethinking Slavery and Reconstruction." *Journal of Negro History,* Vol. 50, No. 3 (July 1965).

Mabry, William Alexander. "Disfranchisement of the Negro in Mississippi." *Journal of Southern History,* Vol. 4, No. 3 (August 1938).

———. "Louisiana Politics and the 'Grandfather Clause.'" *North Carolina Historical Review,* Vol. 13, No. 4 (October 1936).

———. "The Negro in North Carolina Politics Since Reconstruction." *Journal of Negro History,* Vol. 25, No. 4 (October 1940).

_____. "Negro Suffrage and Fusion Rule in North Carolina." *North Carolina Historical Review*, Vol. 12, No. 2 (April 1935).

_____. "'White Supremacy' and the North Carolina Suffrage Amendment." *North Carolina Historical Review*, Vol. 13, No. 1 (January 1936).

Magliocca, Gerard N. *American Founding Son: John Bingham and the Invention of the Fourteenth Amendment*. New York: New York University Press, 2016.

McPherson, James M. "Abolitionists and the Civil Rights Act of 1875." *Journal of American History*, Vol. 52, No. 3 (December 1965).

Menand, Louis. "Morton, Agassiz, and the Origins of Scientific Racism in the United States." *The Journal of Blacks in Higher Education*, No. 34 (Winter, 2001–2002).

Morris, Roy, Jr., *Fraud of the Century: Rutherford B. Hayes, Samuel Tilden, and the Stolen Election of 1876*. New York: Simon & Schuster, 2003.

Nagle, John Copeland. "How Not to Count Votes." *Columbia Law Review*, Vol. 104, No. 6 (October 2004).

Nimmer, Melville B. "A Proposal for Judicial Validation of a Previously Unconstitutional Law: The Civil Rights Act of 1875." *Columbia Law Review*, Vol. 65, No. 8 (December 1965).

Packard, Jerrold M. *American Nightmare: The History of Jim Crow*. New York: St. Martin's Press, 2003.

Perman, Michael. *Struggle for Mastery: Disfranchisement in the South 1888–1908*. Chapel Hill: University of North Carolina Press, 2001.

Pildes, Richard H. "Democracy, Anti-Democracy, and the Canon." *Constitutional Commentary*, Vol. 17 (2000).

Rabinowitz, Howard N. "More Than the Woodward Thesis: Assessing the Strange Career of Jim Crow." *Journal of American History*, Vol. 75, No. 3 (December 1988).

Reed, Thomas B. "The Federal Control of Elections." *North American Review*, Vol. 150, No. 403 (June 1890).

Riser, R. Volney. *Defying Disfranchisement: Black Voting Rights Activism in the Jim Crow South, 1890–1908*. Baton Rouge: Louisiana State University Press, 2010.

Rogers, James Allen. "Darwinism and Social Darwinism." *Journal of the History of Ideas*, Vol. 33, No. 2 (April–June 1972).

Ross, Michael A. "Justice Miller's Reconstruction: The *Slaughter-House Cases,* Health Codes, and Civil Rights in New Orleans, 1861–1873." *Journal of Southern History*, Vol. 64, No. 4 (November 1998).

Smith, George P. "Republican Reconstruction and Section Two of the Fourteenth Amendment." *Western Political Quarterly*, Vol. 23, No. 4 (December 1970).

Spencer, Herbert. *Social Statics*. London: John Chapman, 1851.

———. *Principles of Biology*. Vol. 1. London: Williams and Norgate, 1864.

Stampp, Kenneth M. *The Era of Reconstruction 1865–1877.* New York: Alfred A. Knopf, 1965.

Steelman, Joseph F. "Republican Party Strategists and the Issue of Fusion with Populists in North Carolina, 1893–1894." *North Carolina Historical Review*, Vol. 47, No. 3 (July 1970).

Teel, Steven C. "Lessons on Judicial Interpretation: How Immigrants Takao Ozawa and Yick Wo Searched the Courts for a Place in America." *OAH Magazine of History*, Vol. 13, No. 1, Judicial History (Fall 1998).

Thornbrough, Emma Lou. "American Negro Newspapers, 1880–1914." *Business History Review*, Vol. 40, No. 4 (Winter 1966).

Trefousse, Hans Louis. *Andrew Johnson: A Biography*. New York: W. W. Norton, 1991.

Van Alstyne, William W. "The Fourteenth Amendment, the 'Right' to Vote, and the Understanding of the Thirty-Ninth Congress." *Supreme Court Review*, Vol. 1965 (1965).

Waldman, Michael. *The Fight to Vote*. New York: Simon & Schuster, 2016.

Warren, Charles. *The Supreme Court in United States History*. Boston: Little, Brown and Company, 1923.

Washington, Booker T. *Up from Slavery: An Autobiography*. London: T. Nelson, 1915.

Watson, Douglas S. "The San Francisco McAllisters." *California Historical Society Quarterly*, Vol. 11, No. 2 (June 1932).

Weaver, Valeria W. "The Failure of Civil Rights 1875–1883 and Its Repercussions." *Journal of Negro History*, Vol. 54, No. 4 (October 1969).

Weinberg, Louise. "Holmes' Failure." *Michigan Law Review*, Vol. 96, No. 3 (1997).

Wells, D. Collin. "Social Darwinism." *American Journal of Sociology*, Vol. 12, No. 5 (March 1907).

Wells-Barnett, Ida B. *Lynch Law in Georgia: A Six-Weeks' Record in the Center of Southern Civilization, as Faithfully Chronicled by the "Atlanta Journal" and the "Atlanta Constitution."* Chicago: Chicago Colored Citizens, 1899.

Westin, Alan F. "John Marshall Harlan and the Constitutional Rights of Negroes: The Transformation of a Southerner." *Yale Law Journal*, Vol. 66, No. 5 (April 1957).

White, G. Edward. "John Marshall Harlan I: The Precursor." *American Journal of Legal History*, Vol. 19, No. 1 (January 1975).

Williams, George H. "Reminiscences of the United States Supreme Court." *Yale Law Journal*, Vol. 8, No. 7 (April 1899).

Woodson, Carter G. *A Century of Negro Migration.* Washington, DC: Association for the Study of Negro Life and History, 1918.

Woodward, C. Vann. *The Burden of Southern History.* Baton Rouge: Louisiana State University Press, 1968.

———. *Origins of the New South, 1877–1913.* Baton Rouge: Louisiana State University Press, 1951.

———. *The Strange Career of Jim Crow.* 2nd Edition. New York: Oxford University Press, 1966.

———. "The Political Legacy of Reconstruction." *Journal of Negro Education*, Vol. 26, No. 3, The Negro Voter in the South (Summer 1957).

Wormser, Richard. *The Rise and Fall of Jim Crow.* New York: St. Martin's Press, 2003.

Wyatt-Brown, Bertram. "The Civil Rights Act of 1875." *Western Political Quarterly*, Vol. 18, No. 4 (December 1965).

SOURCE NOTES

Prologue

"It will be the meanest, vilest, dirtiest campaign . . ." Wormser, *The Rise and Fall of Jim Crow*, p. 84.

"Meetings of this kind go on . . ." *Daily Record*, August 18, 1898.

"Last week the editor of the Daily Record of Wilmington . . ." Reprinted in the Wilmington, NC, *Semi-Weekly Messenger*, September 6, 1898, p. 8.

"Why didn't you kill . . ." http://media2.newsobserver.com/content/media/2010/5/3/ghostsof1898.pdf.

"You are Anglo-Saxons . . ." http://media2.newsobserver.com/content/media/2010/5/3/ghostsof1898.pdf.

"White Declaration of Independence" http://media2.newsobserver.com/content/media/2010/5/3/ghostsof1898.pdf.

"Nine Negroes massacred outright . . ." http://www.blackpast.org/1898-rev-charles-s-morris-describes-wilmington-massacre-1898.

"The Men who took down their shotguns . . ." Harry Hayden, *The Story of the Wilmington Rebellion*. (Privately printed, 1936. Reprinted at http://www.1898wilmington.org/hayden.shtml.)

"A German grocer, who knew . . ." https://goinnorth.org/exhibits/show/milo-manly/manly-family.

Chapter 1: Who Votes?

"Viewing the subject in its merits alone . . ." Max Farrand, ed., *The Records of the Federal Convention of 1787*, Vol. 2 (New Haven: Yale University Press, 1937), pp. 203–4.

"Such is the frailty of the human heart . . ." Philip B. Kurland and Ralph Lerner, eds., *The Founders' Constitution* (Chicago: University of Chicago Press, 1987), p. 395.

"under the immediate dominion of others" *Papers of Alexander Hamilton*, ed. Harold C. Syrett (New York: Columbia University Press, 1961–1979), 1:106.

"All communities divide themselves . . ." Max Farrand, ed., *The Records of the Federal Convention of 1787*, Vol. 1 (New Haven: Yale University Press, 1937), p. 299.

"I was for extending the rights of suffrage . . ." *Papers of Thomas Jefferson*, Vol. 1, ed. Julian P. Boyd (Princeton: Princeton University Press, 1950), p. 504.

"Whenever the people are well-informed . . ." https://www.loc.gov/exhibits /jefferson/60.html.

Chapter 3: Two Amendments . . .

"All persons born in the United States and . . ." Statutes at Large, 14 Stat. 27–30.

"a simple, strong, plain declaration . . ." Magliocca, *American Founding Son*, p. 125.

"were being trodden under foot . . ." Johnson said those words to *New York Evening Post* editor Charles Nordhoff, who related them in a letter to William Cullen Bryant. Trefousse, p. 279.

Chapter 4: . . . and a Third: Equal Rights Comes to the Ballot Box

Throughout the old Confederacy . . . Foner, *Freedom's Lawmakers: A Directory of Black Officeholders during Reconstruction*, pp. xi–xxxii.

Chapter 5: Power in Black and White: The Klan

"Insolence to former masters created . . ." Garner, *Reconstruction in Mississippi*, p. 338.

"filled to overflowing the cup of bitterness . . ."; "impossible to conceive . . ."; "The people of the north did not understand . . ." Frank Alexander Montgomery, *Reminiscences of a Mississippian in Peace and War* (Cincinnati: Robert Clarke Company, 1901), pp. 268–270.

"secret political organizations . . ." Garner, *Reconstruction in Mississippi*, p. 338.

"If a party of white men . . ." William A. Dunning, "The Undoing of Reconstruction," *Atlantic Monthly*, Vol. 88 (1901), pp. 440–1.

In the presidential election of 1868 . . . Foner, *Reconstruction*, p. 343.

"it was charged by the Republicans . . ." Garner, *Reconstruction in Mississippi*, p. 341.

Chapter 6: To the Court

"They'll take your . . ." John P. Kaminski and Gaspare J. Saladino, eds., *The Documentary History of the Ratification of the Constitution*, Vol. 10 (Madison: University of Wisconsin, 1990, 1993). Henry's pronouncement was reportedly met with laughter.

"There is no authority that . . ." "Brutus," *To the people of New York* (Antifederalist XV), *New York Journal*, March 20, 1788.

the "people's branch" Alexander Hamilton, James Madison, and John Jay, *The Federalist*. http://avalon.law.yale.edu/subject_menus/fed.asp.

Chapter 7: Any Way You Slice It: The *Slaughter-House Cases*

"indigestible vegetables" or "filthy and . . ." Ross, "Justice Miller's Reconstruction," p. 21.

"a discontented and embittered old man" Quoted in Lane, p. 120.

"that [this arrangement] deprives the butchers . . ."; "An examination of the history . . . balance between State . . ." *Slaughter-House Cases*, 83 U.S. 36 (1873).

Chapter 8: Interlude: Precedent and Politics

"Laws permitting, and even requiring . . . at liberty to act . . ." *Plessy v. Ferguson*, 163 U.S. 537 (1896).

"inherently unequal . . ."; "Does segregation of children . . ." *Brown v. Board of Education*, 47 U.S. 483 (1954).

"that a shotgun having a barrel . . . any part of the ordinary . . . guarantee to the citizen . . ." *United States v. Miller*, 307 U.S. 174 (1939).

"The Second Amendment protects an individual right . . ." *District of Columbia v. Heller*, 554 U.S. 570 (2008).

"a strained and unpersuasive reading." *District of Columbia v. Heller*, 554 U.S. 570 (2008).

Chapter 9: Equality by Law: The Civil Rights Act of 1875

"equal rights in railroads, steamboats, public conveyances . . ." Cong. Globe, 41st Cong., 2d sess., May 13, 1870, p. 3434.

"crown and complete the great work of Reconstruction . . ." Ibid, p. 767.

"whiling away the hours. . ."; "Butler got Sumner's bill passed . . ." Ibid, p. 772.

"All persons within the jurisdiction . . ." Statutes at Large, v. 18, p. 335 (1875).

"It has put us back in the art of governing . . ." *New York Times*, March 2, 1875, p. 6.

"At present, its effect will be mainly political . . ." *Chicago Daily Tribune*, March 1, 1875, p. 4.

"The Supreme Court, in instances such as this . . ." *New York Times*, March 2, 1875, p. 6.

The *Daily Tribune* agreed . . . *Chicago Daily Tribune*, March 1, 1875, p. 4.

Chapter 10: The Uncertainty of Language: *United States v. Reese*

"action required for voting" 16 Statutes at Large 141.

"in any State, Territory . . . to give citizens" 16 Statutes at Large 140–6.

dragged all the way to Louisville . . . Robert J. Kaczorowski, *The Politics of Judicial Interpretation: The Federal Courts, Department of Justice and Civil Rights, 1866–1876* (New York: Fordham University Press, 2005), p. 162.

a "legal mediocrity" and "a weak if not corrupt politician . . ." Ibid.

"It is a wonder that Grant did not pick up . . ." William H. Rehnquist, *Centennial Crisis: The Disputed Election of 1876* (New York: Alfred A. Knopf, 2004), p. 132.

"Mr. Waite stands in the front rank . . ." Widely quoted. See, for example, Lane, p. 231.

"Although his practice has been extensive . . ." *Chicago Daily Tribune*, January 20, 1875, p. 1.

"cold and stoical." Quoted in *Champagne and Pope*, "Joseph P. Bradley," p. 485.

"unconcerned with people . . ." Ibid., p. 482.

"The Fifteenth Amendment confers *no right* . . ." *New Orleans Republican*, June 28, 1874, p. 1.

"The fourteenth amendment prohibits . . ." *United States v. Cruikshank*, 92 U.S. 542 (1875).

"The Fifteenth Amendment to the Constitution does not confer . . ." *United States v. Reese*, 92 U.S. 214 (1875).

Chapter 11: Rutherfraud Ascends, but Not Equal Rights

"white Southerners who sought . . ." Nagle, "How Not to Count Votes," p. 1734.

"Republican Success Certain" *New York Times*, November 6, 1876, p. 1.

"Result Still Uncertain" *New York Times*, November 8, 1876, p. 1.

On election night, Reid convinced local Republican leaders . . . Nagle, "How Not to Count Votes," p. 1736.

"The Battle Won . . ." *New York Times* (hereafter *NYT*), November 8, 1876, p. 1; November 9, 1876, p. 1.

"No one, perhaps not even Davis . . ." Morris, *Fraud of the Century*, p. 168.

"Reasonable men in both parties . . ." Allan Peskin, "Was There a Compromise of 1877?" *Journal of American History*, Vol. 60, No. 1 (June 1973), p. 63.

Chapter 12: The Court Giveth. . . : *Strauder v. West Virginia*

"Horrible Murder . . ." *Wheeling Daily Intelligencer*, April 19, 1872, p. 4. The newspaper was four pages long and, unlike contemporary newspapers, featured the major local news on the back page.

"Afterwards they engaged in . . ." *Wheeling Daily Register*, July 22, 1873, p. 4.

"Not today." *Wheeling Daily Intelligencer*, August 29, 1873, p. 4.

They did so not on constitutional grounds . . . According to statute, the case needed to be put before county court as an examining court before it could be tried in circuit court, and that had not been done.

In early March, one newspaper reported . . . *Wheeling Daily Register*, March 3, 1875, p.4.

"Immediately a colored man came out . . ." *Wheeling Daily Intelligencer*, December 23, 1876, p. 4.

"not whether a colored man . . ."; "The colored race, as a race . . ."; "The very fact that colored people . . ." *Strauder v. West Virginia*, 100 U.S. 303–312 (1880). (Italics added.)

"looking very well . . . dressed neatly . . ." *Wheeling Daily Intelligencer*, May 3, 1881, p. 4.

"Taylor Strauder, known as Andrew E. Strauder, shot and . . ." *Wheeling Daily Intelligencer*, April 27, 1898, p. 5.

"As a result of this long fight against the discrimination . . ." *Wheeling Daily Intelligencer*, June 21, 1898, p. 6.

Chapter 13: . . . and the Court Taketh Away: *Virginia v. Rives*

"To any who have known the conditions existing in backwoods schools . . ." William Eleazar Barton, *Pine Knot: A Story of Kentucky Life* (New York: D. Appleton and Co., 1900).

In mid-November 1877 . . . Details of the crime from *Richmond Daily Dispatch*, December 2, 1878, p. 1.

"as a lawyer, orator, and statesman . . ." Lewis Gravely Pedigo, *History of Patrick and Henry Counties, Virginia* (Baltimore: Genealogical Publishing Co., 1933), p. 191.

"exemplary students bent on . . ." Bruce, *History of the University of Virginia*, p. 112.

"raising a scene of disorder . . ." Ibid., p. 116.

"A member of the Charlottesville bar . . ." https://www.loc.gov/resource /mjm.23_1167_1169/?st=gallery.

"The opinions of the chief architect . . ."; "A rightful secession requires . . ." *The Writings of James Madison*, Vol. 9, p. 495.

"small stir amongst the bar . . ."; "Its substantial effect is to strip . . ." *Richmond Daily Dispatch*, November 22, 1878, p. 3.

"In my own court . . ." *Staunton Spectator*, December 17, 1878, p. 2.

"a flagrant and unconstitutional . . ." *Richmond Daily Dispatch*, November 30, 1878, p. 3.

"a man who either regards all the people . . ." *Richmond Daily Dispatch*, December 10, 1878, p. 2.

"The absurdity of the decision . . ." *New Orleans Daily Democrat*, November 30, 1878, p. 4.

Other articles claimed black criminals *begged* to be tried by a white jury. *Richmond Daily Dispatch*, December 5, 1878, p. 2.

"whether a colored man, on trial . . ." *Brooklyn Daily Eagle*, Monday, October 20, 1879, p. 2.

"a war on State Courts." *Chicago Daily Tribune*, March 20, 1879, p. 2.

"instructed to direct the Attorney-General to institute . . ." *NYT*, January 19, 1879, p. 1.

"It did not assert, nor is it claimed now . . ." *Virginia v. Rives*, 100 U.S. 313, 314 (1880).

He was sentenced to five years' imprisonment . . . *Richmond Daily Dispatch*, June 25, 1880, p. 3.

Chapter 14: Bad Science and Big Money

"We took the government away . . ." *Congressional Record*, Fifty-sixth Congress, first session, pages 2347, 2349.

"the most famous American anthropologist of his day." Menand, p. 110.

"the lowest grade of humanity." Ibid.

"a crude and insolent challenge . . ." Hofstadter, *Social Darwinism*, p. 17.

"It is clear that here is one of the most important . . ." *NYT*, March 28, 1860, p. 3.

By the time Agassiz died in 1873 . . . Darwin's second great work, *The Descent of Man, and Selection in Relation to Sex*, would put the final nail in the polygenist coffin. *Descent*, of course, in ascribing humanity's origins to other primates was to arouse even more controversy than *On the Origin of Species* and supply no shortage of fodder to those who preached racial stratification.

Spencer began with two assumptions. Herbert Spencer, "Progress: Its Law and Causes," *Westminster Review*, Vol. 67 (April 1857), p. 446.

"the multiplication of races and the differentiation . . ." Ibid, p. 447.

"but also state-supported education . . ." Hofstadter, *Social Darwinism*, p. 41.

"A premium on skill, intelligence . . ." Ibid., p. 39.

"survival of the fittest" Spencer, *Principles of Biology*, p. 444.

"became his intimate friend and showered him with favors." Ibid, p. 45.

"The growth of a large business is merely a survival of the fittest . . ." Quoted by Hofstadter in *Social Darwinism*, p. 31.

Chapter 15: Strangling the Constitution: The *Civil Rights Cases*

"a colored person [was refused] a seat . . ." *Civil Rights Cases*, 109 U.S. 3 (1883). The New York plaintiff, William R. Davis, was a twenty-six-year-old employee of a black weekly newspaper, the *Progressive American*, who had been born a slave in South Carolina.

"impeach the patriotism" of those who had implemented the Reconstruction programs, "in their eagerness . . ." Horatio Seymour, "The Political Situation," *North American Review,* Vol. 0136, No. 315 (February 1883), p. 155.

"The wing of the Republican party . . ." Woodward, *Origins*, p. 216. Hayes had left office in 1880 and been replaced by James Garfield. But Garfield had been assassinated and Roscoe Conkling associate Chester Arthur was president.

"On the evening of my initiation . . ." Quoted in Westin, "John Marshall Harlan."

"a flagrant invasion of the right . . ." Ibid., p. 653.

"I rejoice," announced the man . . . Ibid, p. 660.

"Under the law of Kentucky . . ." Ibid, p. 666.

"not invest Congress with power . . ." 109 U.S. 3 (1883).

"It would be running the slavery argument into the ground . . ." Ibid. (Italics added.)

"I cannot resist the conclusion that the substance . . ."; "It is not the words of the law . . ." Ibid. (Italics added.)

"Constitutional provisions, adopted in the interest . . . special favorites of the laws . . . What the nation, through congress, has sought . . . Today it is the colored race . . ." Ibid. (Italics added.)

"the whole matter is now remanded . . ." *NYT*, October 16, 1883, p. 4.

"There was a time when this decision would have created . . ." *Brooklyn Daily Eagle*, October 16, 1883, p. 2.

"A Radical Relic Rubbed Out . . ." *Atlanta-Constitution*, October 16, 1883, p. 1.

"We regret that the judicial authority . . ." *Hartford Courant*, October 16, 1883, p. 2.

The *Boston Hub* charged that the Court had deliberately . . . ; "Our government is a farce . . ." "infamous decision of infamous Chief Justice Taney . . ." All quoted in Weaver, "The Failure," p. 371–2.

"At first I was inclined to agree . . ." Quoted in Westin, "John Marshall Harlan," p. 668.

Chapter 16: The Window Cracks Open: The Curious Incident of the Chinese Laundry and Equal Protection

Calling the Sanitary Ordinance "spiteful and hateful," he wrote, "The equality of protection . . ." *Ah Kow v. Nunan*, 12 F. Cas. at 253, 256–7.

Almost $3 million today. *NYT* obituary, op cit., p. 4.

"to prescribe regulations . . . in favor of the validity of such a statute." *United States Supreme Court Reports*, Vol. 59, pp. 1013–1015.

"The principal objection of the petitioner . . . ***against the class mentioned.***" *111 U.S. 703 (1885)*, (Italics added.)

"It's not rocket science . . . favoritism to all others." *118 U.S. 356 (1886)* 118.

"complied with every requisite deemed . . . nor deny to any *person* within its jurisdiction the equal protection of the laws.'" Ibid. (Italics added.)

Chapter 17: Corrupt Redemption: The 1890 Mississippi Constitution

"It is no secret that there has not been a full vote . . ." Quoted in Mabry, "Disfranchisement," p. 319.

Mississippi would be the first state . . . Ibid.

"There is no use to equivocate or lie about the matter . . ." Quoted in Packard, *American Nightmare*, p. 69.

"The eye of the country is on Mississippi." *Jackson Clarion Ledger*, August 11, 1890, quoted in Perman, *Struggle for Mastery*, p. 70.

And so an extraordinary proposal made the rounds . . . Perman, *Struggle for Mastery*, pp. 81–84.

"The poll tax won't keep 'em . . ." *Collier's*, July 6, 1946, p. 18.

"establish the supremacy of the white race." B. E. H. and J. J. K., Jr. "Federal Protection," p. 1066.

"January 1, 1897, Number of Negro voters . . . White, 29,189; Negro, 0." Ibid.

"There is no half-way ground . . . will disfranchise the mass of black voters." *Raleigh North Carolinian*, January 19, 1899, p. 3.

Chapter 18: The Crusader: *Williams v. Mississippi*

On January 9, 1892, a black laborer named John Gibson . . . United States Reports : cases adjudged in the Supreme . . . Vol. 162, p. 567.

"the great prejudice prevailing against him . . ." United States Reports: cases adjudged in the Supreme . . . v. 162, p. 574.

"was to lay before the colored people . . ." Washington, DC, *Evening Star*, October 31, 1895, p. 16.

"Mr. Jones is a Mississippian by birth . . ." *Washington Bee*, December 21, 1895, p. 1.

"Neither the constitution of Mississippi . . ." *Gibson v. Mississippi*, 162 U.S. 565 (1896).

"In view of the constitution, in the eye of the law . . ." *Plessy v. Ferguson*, 163 U.S. 537 (1896).

"These experiences should have taught . . ." *Greenville Times,* December 12, 1896, p. 2.

"[The Fourteenth Amendment] and its effect upon . . ." *Williams v. Mississippi*, 170 U.S. 213 (1898).

"the negro race had acquired or accentuated . . ."; "The Constitution of Mississippi and its statutes do not . . ." Ibid.

Chapter 19: The Window Slams Shut: *Giles v. Harris*

"to return to the plantation districts . . ." Washington, *Up from Slavery*, p. 160.

"one key moment, one decisive turning point . . ." Pildes, "Democracy," p. 296.

"the great mass of the white population . . ." *Giles v. Harris*, 189 U.S. 475 (1903).

Epilogue

"The harsh fact is that in many places . . ." http://www.lbjlibrary.org/lyndon-baines-johnson/speeches-films/president-johnsons-special-message-to-the-congress-the-american-promise.

With increased participation in the electoral process . . . https://epic.org/privacy/voting/register/intro_c.html.

"Our country has changed," . . . "While any racial discrimination in voting . . ." https://supreme.justia.com/cases/federal/us/570/12-96/#tab-opinion-1970752.

"Throwing out pre-clearance when it has worked . . ." https://supreme.justia.com/cases/federal/us/570/12-96/#tab-opinion-1970752.

"The decision in *Shelby County* . . ." https://www.brennancenter.org/analysis/effects-shelby-county-v-holder.

ILLUSTRATION AND PHOTOGRAPH CREDITS

Photos ©: xiv: Southern Historical Collection, The Wilson Library, University of North Carolina at Chapel Hill; xx: Library of Congress; xxi: North Carolina State Archives, Raleigh, NC; xxiii: Courtesy of New Hanover County Public Library, North Carolina Room; xxvi-xxvii: Library of Congress; 3: The New-York Historical Society; 4-5, 9, 15: National Archives and Records Administration; 22: Library of Congress; 24-25: Bells Mill Historical Research and Restoration Society, Inc., Chesapeake, VA; 28: Library of Congress; 31: Schomburg Center for Research in Black Culture/New York Public Library; 32: Library of Congress; 34: Wallach Division Picture Collection/New York Public Library; 38: Library of Congress; 43: Louisiana State Museum; 44, 45: Library of Congress; 58: Bettmann/Getty Images; 59: Fotosearch/Getty Images; 60: Wallach Division Picture Collection/New York Public Library; 69, 71, 81, 84-85, 86, 90: Library of Congress; 108: Albert and Shirley Small Special Collections Library, University of Virginia; 115: Courtesy of Special Collections, Fine Arts Library, Harvard University; 118: Hulton-Deutsch Collection/Corbis/Getty Images; 122-123: The Ohio State University, Billy Ireland Cartoon Library & Museum; 127, 129, 136: Library of Congress; 144: Everett Collection/age fotostock; 146: George Munday/age fotostock; 155: Daderot/Wikimedia; 158: Library of Congress; 159: Fine Art Images/Heritage Images/Getty Images; 160: Library of Congress; 162: mississippimarkers.com/Brother Rogers; 164: Library of Congress; 168-169: Franklin D. Roosevelt Library/National Archives and Records Administration; 176, 183: Library of Congress; 189: Alabama Department of Archives and History; 192, 199: Library of Congress; 210-211: Associated Press/AP Images; 213: Francis Miller/The LIFE Picture Collection/Getty Images.

INDEX

Note: Page numbers in *italics* refer to illustrations.

ACKNOWLEDGMENTS

I AM VERY MUCH indebted to Scholastic, to David Levithan, Tracy van Straaten, Lizette Serrano, and Emily Heddleson, for their commitment and hard work in bringing both *Stolen Justice* and *Unpunished Murder* to what I believe is the most important audience there could be for books such as these. But mostly my thanks and deepest appreciation go to Lisa Sandell, the kind of editor I would conjure up if I suddenly woke up one morning with magical powers. She is smart, dedicated, passionate, and appreciative; a superb guide, and an even better partner. None of this would have been possible without Charlie Olsen, agent par excellence, who saw the possibilities of work I was burning to do and got it to exactly the right person. He even returns my phone calls. Finally, my profound thanks to Professor Henry Louis Gates, Jr., for his willingness to add his name to a story that needs to be told.

And, of course, to my wife, Nancy, who has the utterly thankless job of putting up with me.

Lawrence Goldstone has written more than a dozen books for adults, including three on constitutional law. His first book on the subject for young adults, *Unpunished Murder: Massacre at Colfax and the Quest for Justice*, received three starred reviews and was named a *Booklist* Youth Editor's Choice.

Goldstone's writing has been featured in the *Boston Globe*, *Los Angeles Times*, *Wall Street Journal*, and *New Republic*, among other newspapers and journals. He lives in Sagaponack, New York, with his wife, medieval and Renaissance historian Nancy Goldstone.